Jane Newdick's
BOOK of
HERBS

SIMON & SCHUSTER
LONDON · SYDNEY · NEW YORK · TOKYO · SINGAPORE · TORONTO

C O N

Cooking with Herbs

PAGES 12-79

Soups

•

Salads

•

Breads and Baking

•

Cheeses, Sauces
and Dips

•

Ice Creams and
Sorbets

•

Cakes

•

Herbal Teas and
Drinks

•

Liqueurs and Cordials

•

Gifts and Preserves

Creating with Herbs

PAGES 80-121

Sachets and Insect
Repellents

•

Pillows, Cushions
and Sachets

•

Herb Essential Oils

•

Pot Pourri

•

Fresh and Dried
Posies

•

Balls, Trees and
Hearts

T E N T S

Decorating with Herbs

PAGES 122-167

Wreaths and Garlands
•
Decorative Herb
Bundles
•
Garden Pots and
Containers
•
Indoor Herbs
•
Wooden Outdoor
Containers
•
Christmas Herb
Decorations

Herbs for Health and Beauty

PAGES 168-201

Bath Oils, Scrubs
and Gels
•
Colognes and
Fragrances
•
Hands and Feet
•
Face and Skin
•
Herbs for the Hair

Herbal Information

PAGES 202-220

Harvesting and
Preserving Herbs
•
A Reference Guide
to Herbs
•
Herb Sources
•
Index
•
Credits

Introduction

The benefits of herbs are almost without limit. As well as providing delightful colour and fragrance in our gardens, they offer a wealth of different flavours for cooking and a whole variety of material for decorating our homes. Throughout the centuries their medicinal and therapeutic qualities have helped to cure illnesses and to lift the spirit, while their spicy aromas and sweet fragrances have been used in beauty preparations and health tonics to make us look good and feel even better.

The Ancient peoples of Egypt, China and India cultivated herbs for their healing properties. The Chinese and Greek civilisations developed systems of pharmaceutical prescription based on the use of plants, cataloguing herbs for their medicinal effect and describing their preparation in detail. By the time of the Romans the culinary delights of herbs were fully appreciated, providing the basis for today's Mediterranean cuisine which combines flavours to produce distinctive and classic dishes.

In the medieval monastery gardens herbs were grown close to the kitchen and infirmary. A variety of herbal ingredients were infused to make alcoholic tinctures and liqueurs, satisfying medicinal requirements and the palate, with the bonus of an inner glow.

Throughout Europe in the 16th and 17th centuries, mixed dried flowers and herbs were widely used in pot pourris to disguise unpleasant smells. Fresh herb posies were carried in an effort to ward off disease, particularly plague. Linen chests were made of cedarwood or impregnated with plant oils to protect clothes from insects and mice. 'Sweet' waters made from the essential oils of herb flowers such as lavender and rose were sprinkled liberally indoors.

The Victorians used dried herbal flowers and leaves in more formal decorative arrangements. At Christmas sweet-smelling garlands and swags were draped across the fireplace, where the warmth of the fire would draw out a variety of aromas to scent the room.

RIGHT: An original display idea, decorative herb bundles are beautiful in their fresh state, but the herbs can still be used and displayed when they have dried.

Angelica

BELOW: Herbs offer wonderful, subtle flavourings as well as pretty decorations for making sumptuous, special-occasion cakes.

Recently we have been rediscovering the wider delights of herbs. We use herbal teas to refresh and relax us, aromatherapy and herbal massage oils to pamper our bodies and a broad range of herbal flavours to add interest to our food.

This book presents a selection of herb-enhanced recipes for dishes and drinks, from soups and salads to cakes and cordials. There are recipes for luxurious herbal bath and skin preparations, from cooling colognes to soothing foot baths. Pot pourris and powder mixtures are included to add fragrance to every room in the house, to scent clothes and repel moths and mice. There are decorations to make for the home, such as wreaths and garlands, posies and trees, as well as creative ideas for displaying growing herbs.

ABOVE: *Herbal wreaths are a traditional and delightful decoration. They can be made from fresh or dried herbs – dried roses in this case – to adorn any room.*

Basil

11

Cooking with Herbs

SOUPS
Pages 14-21

SALADS
Pages 22-31

BREADS AND BAKING
Pages 32-37

CHEESES, SAUCES AND DIPS
Pages 38-45

ICE CREAMS AND SORBETS
Pages 46-51

CAKES
Pages 52-59

HERBAL TEAS AND DRINKS
Pages 60-65

LIQUEURS AND CORDIALS
Pages 66-71

GIFTS AND PRESERVES
Pages 72-79

Soups

Herbs can be the main ingredient of a soup, a subtle additional flavouring or a finishing garnish. Their individuality can provide a new twist to classic soup recipes or become the inspiration for new combinations of flavours and textures. Every cuisine around the world has soups based on herbs, whether they are cool and refreshing cold summer soups or meal-in-a-bowl-type soups for winter days. Herbs are best added towards the end of cooking time. This keeps the taste alive and unspoilt. A few hearty soups benefit, though, from long cooking with a herb, to give them a very full flavour; dried herbs may even be used for their intense taste. Freshly-chopped or snipped herbs make the prettiest garnish, sprinkled over each bowl of soup before serving. This may be an old idea, but it never fails to please the eye and the tastebuds.

Right: Herbs with their highly individual fragrant flavours can be used to create a whole variety of soups for all seasons and occasions. Try introducing different herbs to your standard soup recipes for added interest.

Left: A scattering of freshly-snipped, bright green herb leaves – in this case coriander – makes a classically inviting garnish for any seasonal soup.

Coriander

Gazpacho with Herbs

*T*his classic Spanish recipe is best made at the end of the summer when all the ingredients are plentiful and at their peak. You must use tomatoes which are really ripe and flavourful. If your tomatoes seem to taste rather bland, boost with a very little tomato purée or replace half the iced water with tomato juice. Serve from a large bowl or tureen with some or all of the tasty accompaniments listed below.

750g/1¹/₂ lbs very ripe tomatoes
(skinned, if preferred)
2 sweet red peppers, core and seeds removed
1 clove garlic, peeled
4 spring onions
1 cucumber
6 tbsps olive oil
2 tbsps red wine vinegar
1³/₄ pints/1 litre iced water
Salt and pepper
4 sprigs fresh parsley
4 sprigs fresh oregano
1 sprig fresh mint

Garnishes and accompaniments:
Croûtons fried in olive oil, ice cubes, chopped tomatoes, chopped cucumber, chopped onion, chopped mixed herbs, chopped hard-boiled eggs, stoned black or green olives.

Preparation and cooking time: 30 minutes. Serves 4.

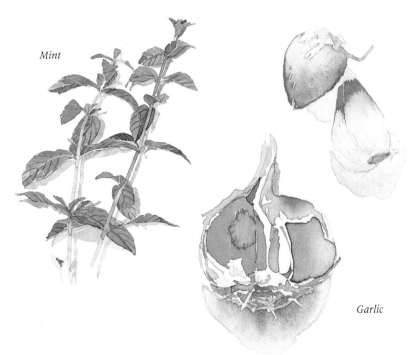

Mint

Garlic

1 Prepare and wash all vegetables and measure the other ingredients.

2 Dice all the vegetables. Tear up the herbs and combine with the vegetables.

3 Blend the vegetables in a food processor until they have a soup-like consistency. Add the oil and vinegar and the iced water until the right consistency is obtained. Season with salt and pepper. Pour into a serving bowl and chill very thoroughly. Serve the garnishes and accompaniments in small, separate bowls from which everyone can help themselves.

Sorrel and Potato Soup

*T*his is a very quick and simple recipe. It can be the basic method for other soups such as a spinach soup, or parsley or watercress could replace the sorrel. The potato gives body and thickening to this healthy and delicious soup.

1 large bunch of sorrel (about 250g/8oz)
1 large potato
20g/1¹/₂oz butter
1 medium onion, skinned
600ml/1 pint chicken or vegetable stock
Salt and pepper
4 tbsps chopped chives
Double cream or crème fraîche

Preparation and cooking time: 45 minutes. Serves 4.

Chives

1 Wash the sorrel carefully. Scrub the potato; there is no need to peel it. Melt the butter in a medium-sized saucepan.

Sorrel

2 *Dice the potato and onion. Shred the sorrel and reserve it. Heat the butter and add the diced onion and potato. Cook over a medium heat, shaking and stirring the contents with a wooden spoon until the onion is transparent but not browned. This will take about 8 minutes.*

Sorrel

ABOVE: Sorrel resembles young spinach leaves in both appearance and flavour, and is cooked in the same ways. This sorrel and potato soup is rich and creamy – ideal for a filling appetiser in the spring or autumn.

3 *Add the sorrel and then the chicken or vegetable stock. Bring to the boil, reduce the heat, cover the pan and simmer gently for about 20 minutes.*

4 *Ladle the soup into a blender or food processor and blend until smooth and creamy. Check the seasoning. Serve each portion with chopped or snipped chives and chive flowers as decoration, and a swirl of double cream or crème fraîche*

Egg, Lemon and Chervil Soup

*T*his is a light and delicate soup, elegant enough for entertaining and a very pretty pale-yellow colour. Use the best ingredients and homemade stock for the best flavour. Chervil is a very subtle and delicious herb with a hint of aniseed. Serve with Melba toast or crisply-toasted pitta bread.

600ml/1 pint chicken stock
Small bunch of chervil
1 lemon, juice squeezed
2 egg yolks
Chervil to garnish

Preparation and cooking time: 20 minutes. Serves 4.

Simmer the stock with the bunch of chervil for about 10 minutes, then strain it. Combine the lemon juice with the egg yolks. Add a ladleful of soup to the egg-and-lemon mixture and return it all to the pan. Reheat, but do not let the soup boil or it will curdle. Whisk over very low heat, just until soup thickens slightly. Serve immediately, decorated with chervil leaves.

Thai Fish Soup with Coriander

*U*se a well-flavoured firm, white fish for this soup, such as monkfish, haddock or cod which will not fall apart during cooking. Eat the soup as the starter to a complete oriental meal or as a main course soup. It is low in fat, very healthy and tastes fragrant and fresh.

750ml/1¼ pints fish stock
1cm/½ inch fresh root ginger, peeled and shredded
250g/8oz firm-fleshed, white fish fillet
About 2 tbsps cornflour
2 egg whites, lightly beaten
3 courgettes
1 lime, rind peeled, to garnish
1 tbsp chopped fresh coriander leaves
A few whole coriander leaves to garnish

Preparation and cooking time: 45 minutes. Serves 4.

Make the fish stock ahead of time, using fish trimmings or a soup cube. Bring to a simmer and add the ginger. Skin the fish fillet if

necessary and cut into small cubes. Dip the cubes into the cornflour, then into the beaten egg white. Transfer the fish to the stock and poach for about 5 minutes, or until the fish is no longer transparent and is cooked through. Do not let the liquid boil. Remove the fish and keep it warm. Slice the courgettes at an angle and cook these in the stock for 8 minutes. Add the lime juice and chopped coriander. Return the fish to the pan to warm it through. Serve decorated with whole coriander leaves and a twist of lime peel.

Coriander

The fragrant combination of coriander and ginger lends character to this fish-based soup. Full of different textures, it would make an interesting main course for a special occasion.

Above: This egg, lemon and chervil soup is ideal for slimmers but tastes hearty enough for no one to suspect just how healthy it is! Serve as a starter before a fish-based entrée. Chervil is a classic French herb and is used much like parsley, but it is more subtle in flavour and needs to be used in quantity.

Salads

Salads these days are all-year-round foods, or should be. They can be a refreshing break between courses, a starter or side-dish, or a complete meal in themselves. A salad can be based around a single ingredient or can be a wonderful, surprising mixture of many different things. Whatever the salad, it is not complete without herbs to add flavour, zest and colour. At one time, salads often contained nothing but a mixture of many different herbs, including the leaves, buds and flowers. We have become less adventurous these days, using herbs only sparingly, but now that we can buy fresh herbs all the year round in great variety, perhaps the herbal salad should be reinstated. Needless to say, the herbs you choose should always be fresh. Dried herbs have no place here, except occasionally in certain dressings.

BELOW: Dare to be different and serve this melon dressed with honey, fruit juices, mint and violet as a refreshing starter. See page 30 for the full recipe.

RIGHT: No salad is really complete without the addition of fresh herbs. Even the simplest dish of salad leaves can become delicious and decorative in this way.

Roast Pepper and Basil Salad

*F*or those who don't like the aggressive taste of raw peppers, this salad is a revelation. Grilling the peppers adds a wonderful smoky, mellow taste and the texture is soft and melting. Serve as a first course or with another salad as a complete meal.

4 yellow peppers
4 red peppers
1 tbsp virgin olive oil
1 tbsp red wine vinegar
Bunch of basil

Preparation and cooking time: 20 minutes. Serves 4.

Basil

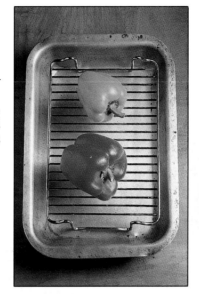

1 *Preheat the grill. Place the peppers whole on a grill pan and grill under high heat. The peppers can also be grilled over a gas flame or in a very hot oven. Turn them frequently. The cooking should take about 5 minutes.*

2 *When the skin is wrinkled and blackened in places, quickly transfer the peppers to a large plastic bag and fold the top over. Leave them in there to cool.*

3 *The skin should now peel off the peppers very easily. Slice the peppers into narrow strips, discarding the inner core, stalk and seeds.*

4 *Arrange the strips prettily on a flat serving dish and sprinkle with the oil and vinegar. Strew basil leaves over the peppers and leave to marinate for an hour or so at room temperature. Do not chill, but eat at room temperature.*

Tricolor Pasta Salad

*T*his salad looks absolutely stunning with its colours of the Italian flag. It is a filling dish, suitable as a summer main course. Serve with Italian breads, a green salad and Chianti to drink. You could vary this recipe by using a different kind of cheese and experimenting with other herbs too.

500g/1¼ lbs pasta spirals (or other pasta shapes)
250g/8oz mozzarella cheese
5 sun-dried tomatoes in oil
125g/4oz black olives
150ml/5fl oz vinaigrette dressing (made with 3 parts
virgin olive oil to 1 part wine vinegar or lemon juice, plus
salt, pepper and a pinch of mustard powder)
5 stems marjoram
3 stems basil

Preparation and cooking time: 20 minutes. Serves 4.

Golden marjoram

1 Cook the pasta in plenty of boiling water until just done, about 12 minutes. Drain the pasta and rinse in plenty of cold water to keep the shapes separate and stop it cooking further. Place it in a large mixing bowl.

2 Cut the mozzarella into small cubes and the sun-dried tomatoes into small strips. Stone the olives, if liked. Mix the dressing ingredients, shaking them in a bottle or blending them in a liquidiser.

3 Snip or chop the marjoram and basil into small pieces. Combine the cooled pasta with the cheese, olives and tomatoes. Add enough dressing to lightly coat the pasta, then add the herbs. Stir well, and leave at room temperature, lightly covered, for about an hour for the flavours to combine. Serve at room temperature.

Strawberry, Goat Cheese and Sweet Cicely Salad

*T*his is a wonderful combination. The touch of sweetness in the dressing harmonises beautifully with the sharp strawberries. You could use any green leaves as the base, but curly endive (also known as batavia or frisée) and oakleaf lettuce look particularly pretty. Use any kind of firmish goat cheese, either individual cheeses or cut from a log.

Preparation time: 10 minutes. Serves 4.

1 curly endive or oakleaf lettuce
125g/4oz strawberries
125g/4oz goat cheese
1 tbsp chopped sweet cicely

Peppermint

For the dressing:
1 tsp honey
Small pinch dry mustard
1 tbsp white wine or strawberry vinegar
3 tbsps oil (olive, sunflower or grapeseed)

Wash and dry the curly endive. Slice the strawberries lengthways. Cut the cheese into small pieces. Whisk the dressing ingredients together and add the sweet cicely. Pour this over the salad and toss well together.

28

Tabbouleh Salad

*V*ersions of this salad appear throughout the Middle East. The parsley and mint are the important ingredients and their taste should predominate; there should be about twice as much parsley and mint as bulgur. Though based on wheat, this salad is light and delicious. It is refreshing and yet sustaining on a hot day. Bulgur, also known as burghul, bulghur, or pourgouri is parboiled, cracked wheat and is now widely available from supermarkets and Cypriot and Asian food shops. Flat-leaved parsley has the best flavour for this dish.

3 ripe tomatoes
¹/₂ cucumber
1 large bunch flat-leaved parsley
1 large bunch mint
4 tbsps olive oil
3 tbsps lemon juice
125g/4oz bulgur
5 spring onions
Salt and pepper

Preparation and soaking time: 2 ¹/₂ hours. Serves 4-6.

1 Wash the tomatoes and cucumber and rinse and dry the herbs. Measure out the oil and lemon juice.

Parsley

2 Put the bulgur into a large bowl and pour plenty of cold water over it. Leave it to soak for two hours; when soft, drain it thoroughly and put it into a serving bowl.

3 Chop the tomatoes and cucumber into small dice and slice the spring onions. Chop the mint and parsley very finely, either by hand or in a food processor. Mix the oil and lemon juice together.

4 Now simply combine everything, stirring really well to distribute the herbs. Leave in a cool place for the flavours to develop for about an hour if possible, but do not refrigerate. Season to taste before serving.

Mesclun

*T*his is a medieval French salad brought up-to-date. The choice of salad leaves is so good these days that it is easy to compose a different salad every day. A percentage of bitter leaves in a salad gives it a delicious edge and is excellent alongside all kinds of other dishes. Or use it as a salad to eat between courses.

Choose from any combination of these ingredients:
Curly endive (also known as chicory, batavia or frisée), radicchio, rocket plant, chicory, cos lettuce, round-heart lettuce, oakleaf lettuce, watercress, endive and lamb's lettuce (mâche).

Add herbs such as lovage, parsley, chives, chervil, tarragon, marjoram, basil, marigold petals and nasturtium leaves.

Use a favourite dressing, spiked with a crushed clove of garlic and a little grainy mustard.

Marigold

Melon with Mint and Violet

*T*his is a refreshing way to eat melon and is more of a dessert than a salad. You could also serve the melon cut into small pieces and tossed with the dressing rather than in its skin.

2 tbsps honey
150ml/5fl oz water
1 sprig mint
150ml/ 5fl oz apple juice
1 tbsp lemon juice
1 tbsp chopped applemint
4 small Charentais or Ogen melons
Fresh violet flowers, to decorate

Preparation time: 20 minutes. Serves 4.

Gently heat the honey in the water until dissolved. Bring to boil, add the mint sprig and simmer for about 10 minutes. Cool, and remove the mint. Combine the liquid with the apple juice and lemon juice. Add the chopped applemint. Slice off the top of each melon and scoop out the seeds. Pour some of the dressing into each melon. Decorate with violet flowers.

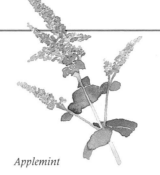

LEFT: Mesclun, a medieval-inspired mixed-leaf salad. Experiment with different combinations of salad leaves, herbs and dressings to create subtle variations of texture, colour and flavour. Choose only the freshest leaves.

Applemint

BELOW: This delightful and unusual melon dish can be served either as an appetiser or as a dessert. Whichever you decide, it is perfect for a hot summer's day.

Breads and Baking

*H*ome baking is fun to do and very rewarding. The results are always a hundred times better than anything which can be bought, and the warm baking smell filling the house is one of life's great pleasures. Herbs can play their part in baking of all kinds, from rosemary-studded Italian focaccia to good old-fashioned cheese-and-herb wholemeal scones. If time is short, then use herbs to jazz up bought breads by wrapping them in foil like garlic bread and heating them in the oven with herb butters. Herb-flavoured breads and scones are wonderful served alongside soups of all kinds or to accompany a salad. Adapt existing recipes that you have for favourite breads by adding fresh or dried herbs. There is little that can go wrong by doing this and you may discover all kinds of fabulous new tastes.

BELOW: The seeds of the caraway plant make an excellent flavouring for breads, cakes and biscuits. The young feathery leaves can be used in soups and salads.

RIGHT: Home-baked breads are a delicious treat made extra special by the addition of fresh or dried herbs. They are also easier and quicker to make than you might think.

Caraway

Rosemary Focaccia

450g/1 lb strong plain unbleached white flour
½ tsp salt
1 tsp active easy-blend dry yeast
About 250ml/8fl oz warm water
About 5 tbsps virgin olive oil
Fresh rosemary
Coarse sea salt

Rosemary

Preparation and baking time: 2½ hours. Serves 10-12.

1 Mix the flour, salt and yeast in a large bowl. Add the water and about 5 tbsps olive oil. Stir with a wooden spoon, then knead with your hands. Turn the dough out on to a wooden board, and knead for several minutes.

2 Return the dough to the bowl, cover with a damp cloth and leave in a warm place until doubled in bulk, about 1 hour.

3 Remove the dough from the bowl and punch it down on a floured board. Shape it into one large or two small circles and make dents all over surface with a wooden spoon handle. Lay the circles on greased baking trays. Cover again and leave to prove. Pre-heat the oven to 220°C/425°F/Gas Mark 7.

4 When the dough has been proving for about 20 minutes, brush the surface with plenty of olive oil and scatter it with rosemary leaves and coarse salt. Bake for 30 minutes, then reduce the heat to 180°C/350°F/Gas Mark 4 and bake for a further 10 minutes. Cool on a wire rack, and brush with more oil to keep the crust soft.

Chilli and Garlic Tortilla Chips

*I*t is very easy to make your own crisp little tortillas and they taste even better than bought ones. Adjust the amount of chilli to suit your taste. Serve them as a snack or to dip into guacamole or something similar. Cornmeal is now available from health food shops and supermarkets, as well as West Indian grocers.

125g/4oz medium or coarse yellow cornmeal
⅔ cup/90g all-purpose (plain) flour
Pinch of salt
1 green chilli pepper, very finely chopped
1 clove garlic, peeled and crushed
1 tbsp olive oil
6 tbsps milk

Preparation and baking time: 30 minutes.
Makes about 40.

Pre-heat oven to 180°C/350°F/Gas Mark 4. Mix the cornmeal with the flour, salt, chilli and garlic. Now add the oil and then the milk, stirring thoroughly until you have a fairly soft dough. Knead the dough on a floured wooden board for a few minutes. Break off small pieces about the size of a walnut in its shell. Roll each of these out to a thin circle. You can cut each circle into quarters if you prefer. Arrange the chips on a greased baking tray. Bake for about 15 minutes. As they come out of the oven, brush each with a little more oil. Store in an airtight tin.

Caraway Rye Oaten Bread

Caraway seeds have been used to flavour breads and cakes for centuries. Although rather out of favour now in the English-speaking world, they seem ready for a comeback. Caraway and rye are a well-tried partnership and no less delicious for that.

Use fresh or dry yeast but not the type of dry yeast that must be mixed directly with the dry ingredients first.

For the first stage:
1 tbsp active dry yeast or 2 tsps fresh yeast
750ml/1¼ pints warm water
2 tbsps honey
4 tbsps molasses or black treacle
225g/8oz strong plain flour
225g/8oz wholemeal flour

For the second stage:
4 tbsps sunflower oil
Grated rind of one orange
3 tsps salt
2 tbsps caraway seeds
175g/6oz porridge oats
425g/1 lb rye flour
285g/10oz wholemeal flour
1 egg, beaten with 2 tbsps water, or 4 tbsps milk, to glaze
2 tbsps caraway seeds or pinhead oatmeal for topping

Preparation and baking time: 4 hours.
Makes 2 loaves (about 30 slices).

*F*or the first stage, mix the yeast with the warm water, honey and molasses or treacle. Add the flours and stir for a few minutes. Cover and leave for about an hour or until foaming. For the second stage, add the oil, orange rind, salt and caraway seeds to the mixture. Stir in the oats and rye flour. Now start to add the wholemeal flour. As the dough gets drier, turn it out of the bowl and knead in more flour, until you have a stiff elastic dough. Knead for several more minutes. Cover the dough and leave it to rise for an hour. Knead again, then cut into two and shape into two round loaves. Glaze with egg or milk if you like and scatter caraway and/or pinhead oatmeal on top. Pre-heat the oven to 220°C/425°F/Gas Mark 7. Leave the dough to prove for about 40 minutes. Slash the surface of the loaves and bake for about an hour or until golden-brown and sounding hollow when tapped. Cool on a wire rack.

RIGHT: Caraway and rye bread is pictured here in the background, with cheese and thyme scones in the foreground.

Cheese and Thyme Scones

*U*se a full-flavoured cheese for this recipe. These scones may not be as light as conventional white ones but they are delicious if split and filled with butter and eaten warm. Fresh thyme is best but you could use the dried herb, in which case use half the amount given.

250g/8oz wholemeal self-raising flour
Pinch of mustard powder
Pinch of cayenne pepper
125g/4oz Cheddar cheese
50g/2oz butter
1 egg, beaten
1 tsp finely chopped fresh thyme
4-5 tbsps milk

Preparation and baking time: 45 minutes.
Makes about 15.

1 Sift the flour, mustard and cayenne together. Pre-heat the oven to 200°C/400°F/Gas Mark 6. Grate the cheese, reserving a quarter of it to sprinkle over the scones before baking.

2 Cut the butter into small pieces and add to the flour mixture. Rub the butter into the flour until the mixture resembles breadcrumbs.

3 Add the beaten egg and thyme to the dough and stir in the milk and the cheese with a fork. The dough should be soft but not wet. Turn it out on to a lightly-floured board and pat lightly into a flat shape about 3cm/1 inch thick. Do not overhandle it. Use a biscuit cutter to cut out scones from the dough. Re-roll and cut more from the scraps.

4 Arrange the scones on the greased baking tray and brush them with a little milk. Scatter the reserved cheese over the scones, plus a little more thyme. Bake in a hot oven for about 15 to 20 minutes. Cool on a wire rack; eat while still warm.

Thyme

Cheeses, Sauces and Dips

*H*erbs really come into their own when combined with the soft textures and bland flavours of most cheeses, sauces and dips. A plain mayonnaise is transformed by the addition of plenty of chopped, fresh herbs such as tarragon, basil, watercress or sorrel. You can also make purées of single herbs, bound with a little oil, to be added to soups, stews and sauces of all kinds. These mixtures can be stored in small pots and refrigerated for several days. If you have time, pound the herbs with a pestle in a mortar rather than using a food processor. The slower process seems to release more flavour and essential oils, as the leaves are bruised rather than chopped. They also keep their colour better.

Cheeses blended with herbs are usually expensive to buy and yet they are so easy to make at home, and taste much fresher and better too at a fraction of the cost. All kinds of soft, fresh cheeses can be used, depending on local availability, made from cow's milk, goat's milk or ewe's milk.

ABOVE: Garlic and chives make an ideal partnership as a flavouring for this creamy cheese spread, which tastes delicious with home-made breads, crackers or biscuits. See page 43 for the recipe.

RIGHT: Label and date jars of herb purées in oil as you store them in the refrigerator for easy identification and to ensure that you do not keep the mixtures longer than a few days.

Mustard and Dill Sauce

*T*his delicious cold sauce is the classic accompaniment to gravlax or gravadlax, the pickled salmon dish which has become so popular outside its native Scandinavia. It goes well with all kinds of smoked or pickled fish, including smoked salmon, and keeps well in the refrigerator for several days. Dill is a pretty, feathery-leaved annual herb with the flavour of fennel. The sauce is not as thick as plain mayonnaise. If you are nervous about using raw egg yolks, use 25g/1oz of tofu instead.

1 egg yolk or 25g/1oz tofu
2 tbsps French mustard
1 tbsp sugar
150ml/5fl oz sunflower oil
2 tbsps white wine vinegar
Bunch of fresh dill
Salt and pepper

Preparation time: 15 minutes. Serves 4.

1 Such a small amount is best made in a mortar or small bowl. Measure out the ingredients and put the sunflower oil into a small jug for pouring it into the mixture drop by drop.

Parsley

Dill

2 Combine the egg yolk or tofu, mustard and sugar together and a dash of the vinegar.

3 Now add the oil, drop by drop, whisking as you go. Once you have incorporated about half, you can pour in the rest in a steady stream until you have a smooth sauce. Add the vinegar and taste the mixture.

4 Season with salt and pepper and add the chopped dill, mixing it in well. Taste again and adjust the seasoning and herbs if needed. Store in the refrigerator.

RIGHT: The subtleness of dill with its aromatic but sweet flavour makes it a perfect partner for fish. This mustard and dill sauce is the ideal accompaniment to pickled, smoked or barbecued salmon.

Pesto Sauce

Basil

Pesto has become a very popular sauce these days. It is used not just with pasta or soups, but is finding its way into all kinds of dishes. Home-made versions are far and away better than the bought variety but you will need a source of plenty of fresh basil to make it worth doing. Store it for a day or so in the refrigerator or freeze batches of it for use later. If you have the patience, make this using a pestle and mortar, but you could use a food processor instead.

40 leaves of fresh basil
2 garlic cloves
Coarse salt
50g/2oz pine kernels
2 tbsps grated Parmesan cheese
240ml/8fl oz extra-virgin olive oil
Salt and pepper (optional)

Preparation time: 15 minutes. Serves 4.

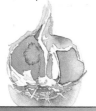

Garlic

1 Pull the leaves from the stems of the basil and tear into small pieces. Peel the garlic cloves.

2 Put the basil, garlic and pinch of coarse salt into the mortar and start to pound the leaves, pressing against the sides of the bowl.

3 Add the pine kernels, and continue to pound until they are crushed. Then add the cheese and stir well.

4 Begin to add the oil drop by drop, pounding continuously, until you have a good, creamy texture. Season, if liked, with salt and pepper.

Garlic and Chive Soft Cheese

*T*his is reminiscent of a certain well-known French cheese. It is worth blanching the garlic so that it doesn't taste so fiery. Any bland soft cheese, from full-fat cream cheese to very low fat curd cheese, can be used. It should have a fairly stiff consistency.

1 clove garlic
Pinch of salt
1 tbsp chopped parsley
1 tbsp snipped chives
225g/8oz fresh soft cheese
Salt and pepper

Preparation time: 20 minutes. Serves 4.

Peel the garlic and blanch in boiling water for about 3 minutes. Now crush the garlic with a pinch of salt. Beat the garlic and herbs into the cheese. Taste and add more salt if needed, and a little pepper. Pile the mixture into a small dish and chill for several hours. Serve with plain biscuits or crackers.

Soft Cheeses Rolled in Herbs

*Y*ou can use almost any rindless soft, white cheese which is stiff enough to withstand kneading and rolling into shape. Try to avoid very heavily-salted soft cheese, or those that are too crumbly in texture. Goat's milk cheeses of all kinds are delicious when given this herbal treatment. Wrap some of the cheese shapes in vine leaves and leave for several hours to absorb their distinctive flavour.

Quantities will depend on how much you wish to make. Tying the cheeses with strips of herb or lengths of chive looks very pretty too. Tuck in a fresh edible flower (a pansy or nasturtium, for instance) as well for a really decorative overall effect.

Preparation time: 15 minutes.

Tarragon

1 You will need a quantity of fresh soft cheese and different herbs such as sweet cicely, chervil, chives, parsley, tarragon, etc.

Chives

2 Using your hands and a knife, shape the cheese into small round, flattened cakes. Prepare the herbs you have chosen by chopping or snipping them into tiny pieces. Using a food processor would badly bruise many herbs, such as chives, so they are best snipped with scissors.

3 Put the herbs on a flat plate. Roll and pat the herbs on to the cheeses, then transfer to another plate, cover with muslin or a kitchen towel and chill until needed.

Ice Creams and Sorbets

The aromatic and sometimes pungent flavours of herbs are very successful when used in all kinds of frozen desserts. Herbs with a mint, lemon, orange or rose scent are especially good, since they combine well with the sweetness and creaminess of many of these iced delights. Stronger, more savoury herb flavours make deliciously sharp and surprisingly tasty water ices and sorbets. The way to get really good herb flavours in both ice creams and sorbets is always to use fresh leaves, and to be generous with them. Most recipes require infusing the herbs in a hot or cold syrup or custard which absorbs the flavour of the herb and becomes the basis of the sorbet or ice cream. Sometimes additional fresh herbs are chopped finely and added to the mixture before freezing. It is perfectly possible to make satisfactory frozen desserts by freezing them in the freezing compartment of the refrigerator and stirring them every so often to break up the crystals, but an ice-cream maker produces the best and creamiest textures. It is also so much more convenient, of course.

Rose

FAR RIGHT: *Herb-flavoured ice creams and sorbets not only taste wonderful but they also look gorgeously tempting, decorated with delicately-coloured herb flowers. Always use fresh herbs and in generous amounts to achieve the best flavours in these cool desserts.*

46

Rose Petal Ice Cream

*T*his ice cream is indulgently delicious. The pale pink colour is inviting and the taste subtle and scented. It looks particularly impressive if served in a pastry case made of sweet shortcrust dough. It can also be eaten alongside soft summer fruits such as raspberries, cherries and strawberries, in season with the roses. Use highly-scented rose petal varieties from a garden rose which is either deep pink or red, and make sure that you use flowers that have not been sprayed.

375ml/12fl oz whipping cream
125ml/4fl oz full-cream milk
4 scented roses
2 egg yolks
75g/3oz white sugar
2 tsps runny honey
2 drops pink food colouring

Preparation and freezing time: 2¹/₂ hours. Serves 4-6.

1 Put the cream, milk and rose petals in a saucepan and bring to just below the boil. Remove from the heat, cover and leave to infuse until cool.

2 Whisk egg yolks, sugar and honey together in a large metal or china bowl until pale and creamy.

3 Strain the rose-flavoured milk into the egg mixture and return to the pan, or put the bowl over a pan of boiling water. Cook very gently until slightly thickened, but do not let it boil. Add a drop or two of colouring.

4 Chill the custard mixture, then freeze it or process it in an ice-cream maker. Store in the freezer. Leave the mixture to soften from frozen for about 20 minutes to serve.

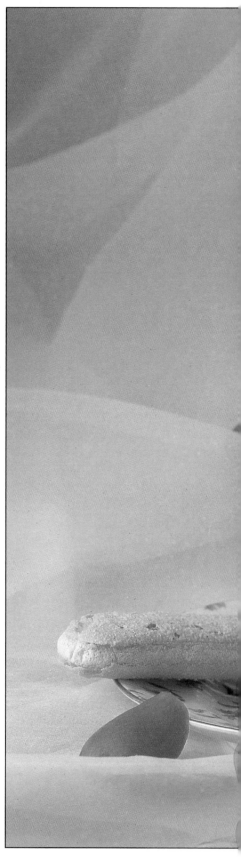

Apricot and Marigold Ice Cream

*I*n early summer, when marigolds are in flower and apricots in season, try this lovely golden-orange ice cream. Make sure you use unsprayed marigold flowers that are recommended for eating, such as the Tangerine Gem or Lemon Gem varieties. Serve with almond biscuits.

500 g/1¼ lbs fresh ripe apricots
1 vanilla pod
75g/3oz sugar
150ml/5fl oz water
150ml/5fl oz double cream
3 marigold heads

Preparation and freezing time: 2¹/₂ hours. Serves 8.

Halve the apricots and stone them. Put them with the vanilla pod in a heavy-based pan with 1 tbsp water. Cover and cook very gently. You could do this in a low oven instead. When cooked, discard the vanilla pod. Purée the fruit, then sieve it. Dissolve the sugar in the water over medium heat in a heavy-based pan. Bring to the boil and cook for 10 minutes to make a thick syrup. Pour this into the purée and leave to cool. Whip the cream and fold this into the mixture. Strip the marigold petals from the flower heads and add these to the mixture. Process in an ice-cream maker or freeze in the freezer or in the freezing compartment of the refrigerator.

Lemon Thyme Sorbet

*A*ll herb sorbets are generally based on a lemon-flavoured sugar syrup. You can add a stiffly-beaten egg white at the stage where the sorbet is nearly frozen. If beaten then, it will whip into a snowy, light texture rather than the more grainy, icy version you get without the egg white. If you are nervous about using raw egg whites, you can now buy dried, pasteurised egg whites as an effective substitute.

125g/4oz caster sugar
450ml/15fl oz water
Juice and thinly pared rind of two lemons
25g/1oz fresh lemon thyme

Preparation and freezing time: 2¹/₂ hours. Serves 4.

1 Put the sugar, water and lemon rind into a heavy-based saucepan and allow the sugar to dissolve without stirring. Bring to the boil, and boil briskly for 5 minutes.

2 Remove the pan from the heat and hold the base briefly under cold water to stop the cooking process. Add the thyme leaves to the syrup, and leave to cool completely.

LEFT: A sumptuous sundae of different herb-flavoured ice creams and sorbet topped with mint and redcurrants. For a special occasion, decorate the glass with a trail of ivy and pin or glue on a single rose flower head.

Lavender Ice Cream.

Lavender

*T*his might sound strange at first, but the subtle use of scented lavender flowers produces a delicate ice cream with an unusual flavour. It is simple to make, using the classic egg custard base, enriched with cream. Serve it with tiny biscuits, such as tuilles, miniature macaroons or wafer biscuits. Ensure that the flowers are unsprayed.

4 egg yolks
75g/3oz white sugar
200ml/6fl oz full-cream milk
6 fresh lavender flower heads
200ml/6fl oz whipping or double cream

Preparation and freezing time: 2¹/₂ hours. Serves 4.

Whisk the egg yolks and sugar together until light and foaming. Gently heat the milk in a pan with the lavender flowers. Bring to the boil, then strain into the egg yolk mixture. Return the mixture to the stove and cook over very low heat, stirring constantly until it is slightly thickened and will coat the back of a spoon. Do not let it boil. Pour the custard into a bowl and refrigerate until it is completely cold. Whip the cream just until it forms peaks and fold it into the cold custard. Process in an ice-cream maker or freeze in a container in the freezer compartment of the refrigerator. Serve with thin, crisp biscuits.

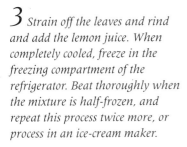

Lemon thyme

3 Strain off the leaves and rind and add the lemon juice. When completely cooled, freeze in the freezing compartment of the refrigerator. Beat thoroughly when the mixture is half-frozen, and repeat this process twice more, or process in an ice-cream maker.

Right: Lavender ice cream is delicately-flavoured and prettily-coloured. For even greater eye-appeal, garnish with sprigs of lavender. In fact, all kinds of desserts can be decorated with lavender to great effect.

Cakes

If it seems odd to use herbs as an ingredient for cakes, biscuits and confectionery, think of the flavour of peppermint which is used so successfully in all kinds of sweets, cakes and puddings. It is often forgotten that this flavour originates from a herb plant. We are very unadventurous these days in the way in which we use herbs compared with the cooks of centuries ago, who combined flavours in recipes which seem to us surprisingly modern. Medieval kitchens put herbs in both sweet and savoury dishes as a matter of course. The Victorians made use of herbs to flavour sweet dishes, particularly those based around cream, milk and eggs. A plain sponge cake or custard would be baked in a tin into which was tucked a sprig or two of sweet geranium, a bay leaf or some lemon verbena. Just a faint hint of rosemary or lavender, for example, really enhances a simple pound cake.

Bay

Lemon verbena

RIGHT: Rediscover the culinary skills of the past and add herbs to your list of ingredients when making cakes, biscuits or confectionery; you will be delighted with the different flavours they create.

Sweet Geranium and Rose Layer Cake

*T*his is a spectacular layer cake for a summer party. You could use any red berries in place of the sharp redcurrants to contrast well with the creamy filling and light sponge layers. Dust the surface with icing sugar and decorate with clusters of frosted redcurrants and frosted geranium leaves.

For the cake mixture:
4 eggs
150g/5oz icing sugar
75g/3oz plain white flour
25g/1oz cornflour
$^1/_2$ tsp baking powder
5 rose-scented geranium leaves, chopped very fine

For the filling:
425ml/15fl oz whipping cream
50g/2oz sifted icing sugar
10 pink rose petals, finely chopped
125g/4oz redcurrants
Extra frosted redcurrants and geranium leaves for decoration

Preparation and baking time: 45 minutes. To serve 6-8.

Preheat the oven to 180°C/350°F/Gas Mark 4. Separate the eggs and put the yolks into a large bowl with the icing sugar. Whisk until light, fluffy and pale in colour. In a separate bowl, whisk the egg whites until stiff, then fold them carefully into the yolk mixture. Sift the two flours and baking powder together and add the geranium leaves. Gently fold the flour into the egg mixture. Grease a 20cm/8 inch round springform cake tin and line the base with non-stick baking paper. Spoon the mixture into the tin and bake in the centre of the pre-heated oven for about 25 minutes or until the cake is well risen and light brown. Unmould and cool on a wire rack. When completely cold, slice the cake into three layers. To make the filling, whip the cream until stiff. Fold in half the sugar and the rose petals. Finally fold in the berries. Spread one half of the filling over the bottom layer, lay the middle layer over it and spread with the rest of the filling. Place the top layer on the cake and decorate it with the rest of the icing sugar, sifted over the cake, and the berries and leaves. Chill until required.

RIGHT: A sweet geranium and rose layer cake makes a glamorous centrepiece for a summer celebration. Follow the method opposite to frost the redcurrants.

Frosted Geranium Leaves

Choose small prettily-shaped, scented geranium leaves to frost with sugar (icing or caster) and use as a decoration for cakes and desserts. You can also frost mint leaves and, of course, all kinds of flower petals such as rose and violet petals.

Preparation time: 15 minutes (for 20 leaves). Serves 4.

1 Make sure the leaf is dry and leave some stalk in place. Beat an egg white with a fork until bubbly but do not whisk it. With a fine paintbrush, paint the egg white all over the surface of the leaf, front and back, to completely cover it.

2 Quickly dip the leaf in and out of a pile of sugar on a plate, and shake it so that too much sugar does not stick to the leaf all at once. It is sometimes easier to sprinkle the sugar over the leaf from a spoon or your fingers. Make sure that the whole leaf is covered in sugar.

3 Transfer the sugared leaf to a cake cooling rack or wire mesh tray and stand this somewhere warm and dry until the leaf has hardened and turned crisp, and the sugar is completely dry.

Rose geranium

55

Applemint Angel Food Cake

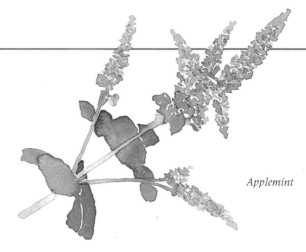

Applemint

*A*ngel food cake is a popular American cake that is feather-light and pure white. It is normally made in an angel food cake tin, which looks something like a charlotte mould. The tin is used exclusively for the purpose and is never greased. If you do not have such a tin, try and use a cake tin with a non-stick surface and do not grease it.

125g/4oz plain flour
25g/1oz cornflour
5 large egg whites
150g/5oz sugar
Grated rind of half a lime
1 tbsp finely chopped applemint

Preparation and baking time: 45 minutes. Serves 6.

Pre-heat the oven to 180°C/350°F/Gas Mark 4. Sift the flour and cornflour with 1 tbsp of the sugar. Whisk the egg whites until stiff, then add the rest of the sugar gradually, whisking until the mixture is very thick. Fold in the flour, grated rind and mint. Line the base and sides of a 20cm/8 inch angel food cake tin, charlotte mould or deep cake tin with non-stick baking paper, or use a non-stick surface. Bake the cake for 35 to 40 minutes. Unmould on to a wire rack, but leave it in the tin until cold. Serve sprinkled with icing sugar. The cake should be eaten soon after baking, as it does not keep well.

Violet Meringues

*T*hese deliciously scented meringues can be sandwiched together with whipped cream. You could add a little violet-scented liqueur, such as Strega, to the cream filling for a special occasion and decorate them with sprigs of mint, sweet geranium or, if in season, purple violas or fresh violets.

3 egg whites
175g/6oz caster sugar
40g/1¾oz crystallised violets
Mauve natural food colouring (optional)
150ml/5fl oz whipping cream
2 tbsps icing sugar (optional)

Preparation, baking and cooling time: 3 hours 45 minutes.
Makes 10 meringues.

1 Line a baking tray with non-stick baking paper. Pre-heat the oven to 140°C/275°F/Gas Mark 1.

2 Put egg whites into a large bowl that is free of grease. Whisk them until they form stiff peaks.

3 Whisk in the sugar 1 tablespoon at a time. Fold in the crystallised violets and colouring, if using. Take two tablespoons and shape the mixture into small ovals. Transfer these to the baking tray. Bake for about 1 hour, then turn the oven off and leave to cool for 1 hour. After an hour, wedge the oven door open with the handle of a wooden spoon and leave until completely cooled, about another hour. Remove the meringues from the oven. Whip the cream until stiff with icing sugar, if liked, and sandwich the meringues together using the filling.

Mint

Viola

Angelica Cake

This rich, buttery cake contains small pieces of candied angelica. You can bake it in a springform tin, a long loaf tin or even a ring mould or savarin tin. It is excellent when eaten quite plain but you could ice it with a lemon-flavoured buttercream or a simple glacé icing. If you have home-made candied angelica (see page 79 for a recipe) then it will taste even better.

4 egg yolks
160ml/5½fl oz sour cream or crème fraîche
100g/3½oz candied angelica
250g/8oz caster sugar
150g/5oz self-raising flour
100g/3½oz plain flour
½ teaspoon bicarbonate of soda
Pinch of salt
170g/6oz softened unsalted butter
½ teaspoon vanilla essence

Preparation, baking and cooling time: 1½ hours. Serves 8-10.

Angelica

1 *Line a cake tin with non-stick baking paper if it does not have a non-stick surface; thoroughly grease the tin. Put yolks into a bowl with 2 tbsps of sour cream and beat well. Finely chop the angelica.*

2 *In a large mixing bowl combine the sugar and flours, bicarbonate of soda and salt. Add the softened butter, the rest of the cream and the vanilla essence.*

3 *Mix thoroughly, beating to incorporate air. Now gradually add the egg mixture, beating well between each addition.*

4 *Fold in the candied angelica. Transfer the mixture to the prepared tin and bake at 180°C/350°F/Gas Mark 4 for about 45 minutes.*

5 *Let the cake cool in the tin for 20 minutes, then turn out on to a wire rack.*

Herbal Teas and Drinks

Soothing warm herb teas or refreshing summer drinks, sophisticated tisanes and spirited wine cups all derive their taste and character from herbs. A herb tea is as simple as can be. Boiling water is poured over fresh or dried herbs and left to infuse. The strained liquid makes a soothing bedtime drink, an after-dinner digestive or an instant pick-me-up, depending upon the herbs used. Chamomile is a good relaxant, whilst peppermint aids digestion and many infusions combine healing properties with their relaxing properties.

Herbs can be used as a decoration for many drinks and as a flavouring for an already distinctive mixture. Imagine mint julep without the mint or a Pimms without the borage! In Victorian times, light wine cups were made for summer parties and outdoor events and they invariably included herbs for flavouring and elegance. Sweet woodruff added its special scent to claret cup and for the children and non-drinkers, ginger mint might embellish a fizzy ginger beer. Lemon balm makes a delicious addition to home-made lemonade but just a sprig will enliven the bought kind too. Flavoured and scented teas are easy to make and are excellent as gifts. Always use a good loose-leaf Indian or China tea as the basis and then experiment, adding flowers and leaves to make your own special blends.

BELOW: Herb teas vary widely in flavour depending on the herbs used, some naturally sweet while others more bitter.

RIGHT: Herb teas have long histories as medicinal cures. They can soothe, calm or invigorate, depending on the particular herb used.

Rose Petal Tea

*F*lower-flavoured teas are quite widely available these days, but it is economical and fun to make your own. As with most China teas, these are meant to be drunk without milk and are suitable for drinking at teatime with sweet foods or as the perfect accompaniment to Chinese or other oriental meals.

2 tbsps scented dried rose petals (pink or red)
125g/4oz black China tealeaves (such as Oolong or Keemun)

1 *If the roses are complete dried heads, then strip off the petals and use just the largest outside ones. Measure out the tea.*

2 *Scatter the petals over the tealeaves and stir them together.*

3 *Pack the tea into suitable containers for storing or to give away as gifts. Little wooden or cardboard gift boxes are ideal.*

4 *To present the box of tea as a gift, add a soft ribbon bow and finish off with a single dried rose as decoration.*

Make jasmine, hibiscus or orange blossom tea in exactly the same way. Jasmine has a strong scent, so use half the quantity that you would for rose petals, mixed into the same amount of tea. You may need to experiment and taste until you have the proportions that you like, as dried flowers vary in their scent and flavour, depending on origin and age.

Three Herb Teas

Chamomile

Make tisanes and herbal teas just as you would make normal Indian or China tea. If you are making a single cup, then invest in a small metal infuser which you fill with a spoonful of the herb and put in a cup. Boiling water is poured over the infuser, which is left for a minute and removed when the herb tea is the right strength. Otherwise, use a small teapot kept just for herb teas, and use a spoonful or so per person. Chamomile makes a light-golden tisane, red sage and melissa are darker and good for sore throats and coughs. Jasmine tea is highly-scented and just right to drink with strong and spicy foods or after a meal.

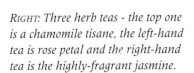

RIGHT: Three herb teas - the top one is a chamomile tisane, the left-hand tea is rose petal and the right-hand tea is the highly-fragrant jasmine.

Lemon Balm Lemonade

*T*his is a version of a simple lemonade but with the extra flavour of lemon balm. This herb is easy to grow and establishes large clumps where it is happy. It can seed itself too prolifically around the garden though, but when in flower the white blooms attract clouds of bees so it is a lovely plant to have. Serve this drink well-chilled to adults and children. Some people may wish to sweeten it further.

4 unsprayed lemons
Small bunch of lemon balm
125g/4oz sugar
150ml/5fl oz boiling water
600ml/1 pint water
Lemon balm sprigs to decorate

*Preparation and chilling time: 1 hour 45 minutes.
Makes about 1 litre/1³/₄ pints.*

1 Scrub the lemons well before peeling off the rind carefully, avoiding as much of the pith as possible.

Lemon balm

2 Put the lemon rind in a small heatproof jug. Tear off the lemon balm leaves and add these with the sugar. Pour the boiling water over this and stir well, crushing the balm leaves to release their flavour. Leave this mixture to infuse.

3 Cut lemons in half and squeeze out the juice. Put a few fresh sprigs of lemon balm into a large glass jug, then strain lemon juice into the jug and add the cooled, strained syrup. Top up with the rest of the water or half-water, half-ice and leave to chill until needed.

Sweet Woodruff Summer Cup

Sweet woodruff is a pretty, easy-to-grow herb whose small white, starry flowers bloom in early summer. Once picked, and as the plant dries, it releases a lovely scent similar to that of new-mown hay. It has long been used to flavour summer drinks both alcoholic and soft.

2 tsps white sugar
1 bunch sweet woodruff
Juice of one lemon
Juice of one orange
1 bottle chilled medium-dry white wine
2 tbsps brandy
1 tbsp Cointreau
Small bottle chilled sparkling mineral water or soda water
125g/4oz strawberries
2 small strips cucumber peel

Preparation time: 30 minutes. Makes about 2 litres/3½ pints.

Dissolve the sugar in a little boiling water, along with all but a few sprigs of sweet woodruff. When cool, strain it and pour into a large serving bowl. Strain the lemon and orange juices and add to the bowl. Add the wine, brandy and Cointreau, and top up with the ice-cool sparkling mineral water or soda water. Slice the strawberries and float them on top, along with the strips of cucumber peel and the reserved sprigs of woodruff. Stir well and serve immediately.

LEFT: *A jug of thirst-quenching lemon balm lemonade with a glass of inviting sweet woodruff summer cup - the perfect choice of a non-alcholic and an alcholic drink to offer at a summer party.*

Sweet woodruff

Liqueurs and Cordials

Herbs find their place in all kinds of drinks and liqueurs, no doubt originally in some health-giving or medicinal way, but these days more as a straightforward flavouring. Chartreuse, for example, is just one of the famous liqueurs made commercially which is based around the flavours of several herbs. The recipe has always been kept strictly secret. The French have long made delicious concoctions, flavouring eau-de-vie or brandy with all manner of herbs, leaves, fruits and berries. The process is very simple to copy and the results are invariably better than many home-made wines which are time-consuming to produce and not always successful. You need vodka, gin or brandy as a base to take the flavourings but you can use the cheapest you can find.

Herbs can also be used to flavour syrups and cordials, to be diluted as refreshing summer drinks. Healthier and cheaper than commercial brands, they are also fun to make and what is more, you know what they contain. The best-known of these is that very English drink, elderflower cordial. Country people have always made use of the flowers and fruits of this common plant and the results are delicious. Elderflower 'champagne' is a little trickier to make and often results in broken bottles and sticky pantries! Best to bottle the flavour in a syrup which can then be diluted to your taste or made sparkling with fizzy water.

Hawthorn

RIGHT: Herb liqueurs and cordials are so simple to make and far more interesting in flavour than their commercial counterparts. Look out for attractive bottles in which to store your home-made drinks.

Citrus Herb Liqueur

There are many variations on the theme of herb-flavoured liqueurs. Some are based on just one herb, others are a mixture of many herbs and other flavourings.

Leave the spirit to mature for as long as possible and adjust the sweetness once it is ready. Do this by adding a sugar syrup until it is to your taste, or you may prefer a drier flavour and drink it as it is. The ingredients are approximate here; you may prefer to add more or take some of the flavourings out.

For a one-litre bottle of vodka you will need:
2 cloves
1 unsprayed clementine, well-washed
1 unsprayed lime, well-washed
1 unsprayed lemon, well-washed
2 vanilla pods
2 cinnamon sticks
6 cardamon pods
About 125g/4oz fresh tarragon
1 sprig rosemary

Makes about 1litre/1¾ pints.

1 Stick the cloves into the clementine and put it into a 2 pint/1.15 litre wide-mouthed jar with a screw-top lid.

2 Peel the lime and lemon very thinly, ensuring that as little of the pith as possible adheres to the rind. Add the rinds to the jar.

3 Add the rest of the ingredients to the jar and fill it with vodka. Leave to mature for at least twelve weeks. Then strain, taste and sweeten if liked.

Tarragon

Elderflower Cordial

Store this in clean bottles or jars, preferably sterilised ones, in the refrigerator. Dilute to taste with water, soda water, lemonade or whatever you choose. The muscat-flavoured, lemony syrup can also be used as a sweet sauce for water ices, ice creams or in puddings, or mixed with other drinks and cocktails. Citric acid (sour salt) is available from the international foods section of the supermarket and from Polish and Jewish grocers.

2 unsprayed lemons
200g/7oz white sugar
600ml/1 pint water
6 heads of elderflowers
2 tsps citric acid (sour salt)

Makes about 600ml/1pint.

Scrub the lemons and peel them. Cut them in half, and squeeze and strain the lemon juice. Put sugar and water in a pan and bring to boil. Add the clean, washed elderflowers and simmer for 10 minutes. Add the lemon rind and leave the syrup to infuse until cool. Strain the syrup, then dissolve citric acid in the lemon juice and add to the syrup. Pour into bottles and store in the refrigerator. Dilute to taste.

LEFT: *Elderflowers have a bitter, rather hot taste when eaten raw, but when infused the resultant liquid becomes grape-like in flavour.*

Elder

May Blossom Brandy

*T*his has to be made in late spring when the hawthorn is in full bloom. Pick the blossoms and shake them free of any dust and insects. Avoid washing them if at all possible. Pack the flowers into a wide-mouthed jar and pour a bottle of cooking brandy over them. Dissolve 3 tbsps sugar in a little boiling water and add to the jar. Close the jar and shake it well. Leave in a cool, dark place for about two to three months, shaking the jar occasionally. Strain, taste and sweeten further with sugar syrup or glucose syrup if you wish.

RIGHT: Rose brandy can be served as an after-dinner liqueur but it can also be used as a rich flavouring for cakes, biscuits or ice cream in the place of rum.

Rose

Rose Brandy

Enough scented red rose petals to fill a screw-top jar
Brandy to cover them
Sugar syrup made with 250ml/8fl oz water to
500ml/16oz sugar
More fresh rose petals

Loosely pack the rose petals into the jar and pour the brandy over them. Close the jar and leave it for about one month, shaking it regularly. Simmer the syrup and add about 125g/4oz fresh rose petals to it. Strain and add this to the brandy. Leave for another week, then strain through a piece of clean muslin into a thoroughly-washed bottle.

You can experiment with making all kinds of other flavours of liqueur, using either of the basic methods described above. Many herbs, leaves and flowers can be tried, for example, rosemary, violet, carnation, borage, pennyroyal and the various varieties of mint. At one time, a drink made with young, fresh beech leaves was popular as a version of noyeau or almond-flavoured liqueur.

Gifts and Preserves

*H*erbal gifts are a lovely idea, combining usefulness and giving pleasure and fun to the maker too. Edible presents are always welcome and show special love and care in their making. A little jar of special preserves or jelly is a treat to receive. These days so few people have time to do their own home canning and yet these preserves are always so good. If your garden is overrun with herbs in the summer and early autumn, make several batches of herb jellies throughout the season. Base these on a sharp fruit, such as cooking apples or gooseberries, and preserve them in small jars whose contents can be used more or less at one sitting. During the winter, these preserves are delicious to eat with roast meat and game or cold meat and cheese.

Flavoured oils and vinegars are another simple idea. They couldn't be easier to make, and yet presented in a pretty bottle with a special label, they are in a class of their own compared with the commercial offerings available. You can control the ingredients, so use only the best, which is what will make all the difference to the final result. Chutney-making is a wonderfully creative branch of cooking as the quantities of ingredients are not critical and you can experiment with spices, herbs and flavourings to create your own personal blends.

Other ideas for herbal food gifts are little bunches of bouquet garni made from dried home-grown herbs, strings of home-grown bay leaves or wreaths made from sage or rosemary. Savoury biscuits and snacks are another area where you can customise your favourite recipes with the addition of particular herbs, and packaged in an attractive way they make wonderful gifts especially at Christmastime, when extra food items are always welcome to feed hungry guests.

RIGHT: Herb-flavoured preserves and vinegars, crackers and snacks, make memorable gifts for relatives and special friends, especially when presented in attractive jars crowned with brightly-coloured fabric covers and boxes tied up with decorative ribbon.

Tomato, Red Pepper and Coriander Chutney

*T*his is a lovely warm, red-coloured chutney. Allow it to mellow for a few weeks for the flavours to blend. Adjust the quantities to suit yourself, and adjust the seasonings and flavourings if you want. Preserve it in small glass jars with screw-top lids. These can then be covered with a pretty circle of fabric or neat brown paper tied on with coloured string.

2 cloves garlic
2 tsps mustard seed
500g/1¼ lbs ripe red and/or yellow tomatoes
1 large onion
500g/1 ¼ lbs sweet red peppers
300g/10oz soft brown sugar
300ml/10fl oz white wine vinegar
½ tsp ground ginger
½ tsp paprika
½ tsp turmeric
1 tbsp salt
1 bunch fresh coriander

Preparation time: 2 hours. Makes about 2 litres/3½ pints.

1 Have ready some small clean, screw-top preserving jars. You will need to cook this in a heavy-based, non-reacting saucepan. Peel the garlic cloves and chop finely. Crush the mustard seeds lightly in a mortar.

Coriander

2 Plunge the tomatoes into boiling water and leave for 2 minutes. Remove them and drop into cold water. Now they will peel very easily. Chop them roughly, and slice the onion.

LEFT: This aromatic tomato, red pepper and coriander chutney is a sweet pickle that goes particularly well with stews and pickled meats.

Coriander

Ginger

Poppyseed Cheese Straws

You can use different kinds of cheese in these light, crumbly biscuits, depending on your taste or whatever the storecupboard has to offer. Whatever you choose should have a strong flavour. The cheese straws should be eaten fresh, slightly warmed or re-heated, as an appetizer or with an apéritif.

225g/8oz plain flour
Pinch of salt
Pinch of cayenne pepper
100g/3½oz butter
50g/2oz finely-grated cheddar or other mature cheese
50g/2oz finely-grated parmesan cheese
2 tbsps poppyseeds
2 eggs, beaten

Preparation and baking time: 45 minutes. Makes 40-50.

Sift the flour with the salt and cayenne pepper. Rub the butter into the flour until the mixture is crumbly. Add the cheeses to the mixture and stir well, then stir in half the poppyseeds. Stir in just enough beaten egg to make the dough hold together firmly, reserving the rest. Pre-heat the oven to 200°C/400°F/Gas Mark 6. Transfer the dough to a floured board and knead it lightly. Roll out by hand into sausage-shapes about 5mm/¼ inch thick, and brush with the reserved beaten egg. Sprinkle with the reserved poppyseeds. Slice into sticks about 7.5cm/3 inch long and transfer to a greased baking tray. Bake the cheese straws for about 8-10 minutes, or until just turning golden. Cool on a wire rack. Serve while still warm, or pack into airtight tins lined with greaseproof paper and give as gifts.

3 Put everything except the coriander into the pan and bring slowly to the boil. Simmer very gently for an hour or more, until the chutney is getting thicker and jelly-like. When it is ready, add the chopped coriander and pour it into

the jars, while still hot, leaving a space of 5mm/¹/₄ inch at the top. Wipe the rims of the jars, put on the two-piece lids and screw down firmly. Place the jars on a rack in a deep preserving pan half-full of boiling water, and add enough boiling water to cover the jars by 5cm/2 inches. Cover the pan, bring to a rolling boil and boil for 15 minutes, reducing the heat if necessary. Remove the jars from the boiling water and leave them to cool.

Herb Jelly

*T*his is a basic recipe which can be used as the basis for all kinds of herb jellies. You might like to try thyme, lemon thyme, lavender, rosemary, marjoram, mint, lemon balm, sage or tarragon. Pot it in the smallest jars you can find. This version uses lemon verbena as the basic herbal ingredient.

1kg/2¹/₄ lbs cooking apples (can be windfalls)
About 300ml/10fl oz water
Sugar
Lemon juice
Fresh herbs
White wine vinegar (optional)

Preparation time: 2 hours + overnight straining.
Makes about 1 litre/1³/₄ pints.

1 *Have ready some small clean, screw-top preserving jars. Roughly chop the apples leaving the skin on and include the pips and stalks. Put into a heavy-based preserving pan and add the water. Simmer very* *gently until the apple has collapsed and cooked thoroughly. Ensure that it does not burn or stick to the bottom of the pan.*

Lemon verbena

LEFT: *Herb jellies make wonderful accompaniments to a whole variety of meat dishes. Try teaming different herb-flavoured jellies with various meats and cheeses.*

3 To each 600ml/22fl oz juice add 500g/1lb 2oz sugar, the juice of one lemon and 3 tbsps of chopped fresh herbs. You can also add 1 tbsp of white wine vinegar to, say, a mint or lemon thyme jelly. Put into a heavy-based pan, bring to the boil and boil rapidly until the jelly has reached setting point. Pour it into the jars while still hot, leaving a space of 5mm/¹/4 inch at the top. Wipe the rims of the jars, put on two-piece lids and screw down firmly. Place the jars on a rack in a deep preserving pan half-full of boiling water, and add enough boiling water to cover the jars by 5cm/2 inches. Cover the pan, bring to a rolling boil and boil for 15 minutes, reducing the heat if necessary. Remove the jars from the boiling water and leave them to cool. When completely cold, remove the seals, label and store the jelly.

2 Strain the fruit pulp through a jelly bag or double cheesecloth (muslin). Do not press the pulp, or the juice will become cloudy. Leave to strain overnight or for several hours. Measure the juice.

Sage

Herb Vinegars

Rosemary

A very simple item to make but a really delicious addition to anyone's storecupboard. The choice of herbs is yours. You can also add extras such as garlic, chillies, whole spices and other flavourings to the basic herb. Certain herbs make classic vinegars. Tarragon is famous and invaluable for making certain egg-and-butter-based sauces for fish and meat. Basil is delicious for making into salad dressings, and garlic vinegar has uses throughout the kitchen. Add a drop here or there to sauces, soups, casseroles, stir-fried dishes, and so on. Try using herb flowers too, such as chives or thyme, to give a delicate colour to the vinegar. Other flowers to try are primrose, violet, rose petal, carnation, elderflower, lavender, nasturtium and marigold. Use a very pale white wine vinegar or a cider vinegar as the base, or for more robust flavours use red wine vinegar.

Bring the vinegar to boiling point. Put whole sprigs or leaves of the fresh herb into sterilised, wide-mouthed bottles or jars and pour the heated vinegar over them, leaving a space of 5mm/$^1/_4$ inch at the top. Wipe the rims of the jars, put on two-piece lids and screw down firmly. When completely cold, label the bottles or jars and leave the vinegar to steep in a cool, dark place for several weeks. You will need to remove the wilted herbs which will have discoloured by now and strain the vinegar into clean, sterilised bottles. Add a few more of the fresh herbs or herb flowers for decoration, if you like. The following is an approximate guide to quantities of fresh herbs to use for 600ml/1 pint vinegar: tarragon – 2 stems; basil – 14 tbsps; garlic – 4 large crushed cloves; bay leaf – 10 leaves; elderflower – 300g/3½oz flowers; rose petal – 300g/3½oz petals; lavender – 30g (1oz) flowers.

Candied Angelica

*T*here are several ways of candying angelica at home, but all require boiling it with green leaves to help preserve the green colour. If you do not grow your own angelica, a good confectionery-making or cake-making supplier will have candied angelica in stock. Glucose syrup is available from these sources or from chemists. Candied angelica is expensive, so the homemade variety would make a nice gift.

450g/1 lb savoy cabbage leaves or fresh vine-leaves
450g/1 lb angelica stems, cleaned, trimmed
and cut into 15cm/6 inch lengths
4 tbsps wine or cider vinegar
450g/1 lb sugar
1 tbsp glucose syrup
125g/4oz icing sugar

Preparation and soaking time: 2½ days. Makes 450g/1 lb.

Line a heavy-based pan with a layer of leaves. Cover with a layer of angelica stems, then add another layer of leaves, and so on, until all are used up, ending with a layer of leaves. Add the vinegar to 600ml/1 pint water and pour the mixture into the pan. Bring to the boil, cover and simmer for 2 hours. Remove from the heat, and leave to cool. Discard the leaves; the angelica should now be bright green. Drain it, then transfer it to a large bowl. Add the sugar and glucose syrup to a heavy-based pan with 250ml/8fl oz water. Bring to the boil without stirring, then boil fairly briskly for 10 minutes. Remove from the heat and pour immediately over the angelica. Stir to ensure all the stems are soaked in syrup. Cover the bowl and store in a cool place for 12 hours.

Strain the syrup from the angelica and bring it to the boil again. Boil for 5 minutes, then pour it over the angelica. Cover and leave for another 12 hours. Finally return the angelica, in its syrup, to the pan and bring back to the boil. Simmer for 20 minutes, adding more glucose syrup if it looks like drying out. Remove from the heat and cool on wire racks. Cut the angelica stems into 7.5cm/3 inch lengths. Sprinkle them generously with icing sugar. Store in airtight metal boxes lined with wax paper.

LEFT: *Be sure to tell the recipient of herb vinegars that they should store them in a cool, dark place to preserve their flavour to the maximum.*

ABOVE: *Tarragon vinegar is a classic herb vinegar. Try adding a clove of garlic to steep in the heated vinegar with the herb.*

Angelica

Creating
with Herbs

SACHETS AND INSECT
REPELLENTS
Pages 82-87

PILLOWS, CUSHIONS
AND SACHETS
Pages 88-93

HERB ESSENTIAL OILS
Pages 94-101

POT POURRI
Pages 102-107

FRESH AND DRIED POSIES
Pages 108-113

BALLS, TREES AND HEARTS
Pages 114-121

Sachets and Insect Repellents

Just one of the many properties some herbs possess is their ability to repel unwanted insects. In our neat and centrally-heated homes these days, we are not plagued by infestations of insects in the way that people once were, but clothes' moths may still try and find a way into the closet and at certain times of the year our cats and dogs suffer from fleas. On hot summer days, flies swarm indoors to irritate us and attempt to settle on food and clean surfaces, and most country homes are occasionally visited by mice seeking shelter during the autumn and winter. All these pests have had their herbal repellents in the past and many of the ideas are well worth knowing about, apart from being another pleasant way to bring herbs into the house. Peppermint is supposed to repel mice. The most effective way to use it for this purpose is to put a few drops of peppermint oil on small pieces of cotton wool and tuck them here and there in lofts and attics, or wherever the mice appear to be getting in.

Cedarwood and sandalwood are two classic scents for keeping chests and cupboards fresh and free of insect pests and mice. Perhaps they are not strictly herbs because both come from the wood of full-grown trees. The small chippings are sold to fill sachets. The essential oils can be sprinkled on wooden shapes or used to impregnate wadding to put inside fabric sachets. Clean linens and fabrics, however well stored, can start to smell musty, especially if not kept totally dry, but these two scents help keep them sweet-smelling.

Cedarwood

RIGHT: Keep your clothes smelling sweet and insect-free by placing herbal sachets in your chest of drawers. Fill the sachets with cedarwood or sandalwood chippings for a woodland scent.

Lavender Bottles

Lavender

*T*his is a very old idea which has been revived over the last few years. You will need fresh-cut lavender to make the bottles successfully, as dried lavender is too brittle and the stems will not bend. The lavender will slowly dry and shrink a little. You may need to re-tie the stems together if they shrink too much. Use the bottles in amongst clothes and linen kept in store.

1 You will need a bunch of fresh, long-stemmed lavender, about 16 to 20 pieces. The flowers should just be opening, but not too far advanced or they may drop as they dry. You will also need some strong, fine thread.

3 Bend back each stem individually from the thread to enclose the lavender flowers. Do this in order, working in one direction.

2 Make a bunch of the lavender, and tie the stems tightly just where the flowers finish on the stem. Cut off the surplus thread.

4 When all the stems are bent back, tie them in place with more thread, under the bulge made by the flowers. This creates the bottle-shape. Tie the bottom of the stems with another piece of thread to hold them neatly in place. Decorate the lavender bottle, if you wish, with a pretty ribbon bow.

Southernwood

A Herb Bunch to Repel Insects

A lovely, old-fashioned way to repel moths and other insects is to make a small scented and decorative bunch to hang above a bed, inside a cupboard or wardrobe or on the back of a door. You will need a sprig or two of southernwood (field southernwood or artemisia) which has a strange, bitter scent, several red roses, a small bunch of lavender and one of hyssop. These can be fresh to begin with, or dried. If they are fresh, they will slowly dry out over the space of a few weeks. Make a bunch in your hand, putting the longest-stemmed plants, such as the lavender, at the back. Tie the stems together with ribbon or string.

Insect-repellent Sachets

Make small fabric sachets from scraps or remnants of fabric to hold herb mixtures designed to keep moths away and to scent clothes and linens. You can make bag-shaped sachets which are simply tied together or you can make small, square, flatter sachets which are filled and then sewn closed. The fabric you choose must have a fine enough weave to prevent any of the mixture escaping. A suitable herb mixture to fill these sachets would be based around tansy and southernwood, with rosemary and lavender added. You should be able to buy all these herbs dried from a good herbalist.

The recipe gives proportions of ingredients rather than weights or volumes. This means that you can choose the measure you want according to how much you want to make up.

Tansy

RIGHT: *Tansy and southernwood are the active herbs in repelling moths. Other herbs, such as rosemary and lavender, are added to sachets for their heady fragrance.*

Mint

Herb Sachet Recipe 1

4 measures tansy
4 measures southernwood
(field southernwood or artemisia)
2 measures lavender
1 measure rosemary
½ measure powdered orris root

Mix the ingredients together and use to fill sachets. Orris root acts as a fixative on the herb scents, keeping them fragrant.

Herb Sachet Recipe 2

2 measures santolina
2 measures marjoram
1 measure lavender
1 measure tansy
½ measure orris root powder

Mix all the ingredients together and use as required.

Mint is supposed to keep the flies away so it is a nice custom to hang a small bunch of fresh mint at an open window, or stand a jug of mint stems in water on a window-sill. You could try a bunch of lavender, too, for the same effect. If you do not have the fresh herb, then try dabbing a few drops of the essential oil on to something suitable. Pennyroyal, which is a member of the mint family, has always been used against fleas. It may be worth trying this out by rubbing a pet's coat with the fresh leaves or putting some of the herb in with the animal's bedding. It may just help!

Pillows, Cushions and Sachets

Filling pillows or bedding with sweet-smelling, soothing herbs is an old tradition. When mattresses and beds were made from straw or other plant material stuffed into a linen sack of some kind, it was common to add other dried leaves and plants to keep the bedding smelling sweet and fresh. Nowadays, we might keep the spirit of this idea by putting small scented pillows in amongst a pile of larger ones on a bed, or filling a special pillow with relaxing herbs to leave under a bed pillow to help induce sleep. As when you make smaller sachets, you should use a fabric which will keep the filling from escaping, something smooth and finely-woven, unless you are simply stuffing the cushion with wadding impregnated with an essential oil. Silk, cotton and linen are all natural fabrics and are the most pleasing to use.

One way of introducing scent into a cushion is to make a small sachet which slides into a pocket on the side of a large cushion. This is a practical method, as it means that the little sachet can be removed easily and replenished or changed when needed. Sachets and small pillows can be decorated in all kinds of ways. If you are good at embroidery, embellish your sachets and pillows with decorative initials or motifs, flowers or hearts, or whatever takes your fancy.

The lavender bag is the most popular scented sachet and deservedly so. The fresh, astringent perfume of lavender is always welcome, so be lavish about putting these little bags amongst clothes in cupboards and drawers. Adding a fixative to the dried lavender will help to preserve the scent. At one time, sachets were always filled with a ground mixture of herbs and spices, rather than the mixed leaves and flower petals more commonly used today. These contained fixatives to hold and fix the scent. Sweet powder is fun to make and you can vary the scent according to the ingredients. Experimenting with different spices, for example, can change the character of the scent dramatically from, say, warm and spicy to sharp and fresh.

Thyme

RIGHT: Herb-filled pillows, cushions or sachets are easily made and can be very decorative, trimmed with ribbon or lace, or embroidered.

Sweet Powder Mixture 1

Thyme

This recipe is measured out in volume rather than weight. Use whatever size of measure you feel you need according to the amount of mixture you wish to make. A cupful (250ml/8fl oz) is a good size to base it on.

You really do need a spice- or coffee-mill to make this successfully, though you could buy the spices ready ground and just crumble the larger leaves. It would be advisable to keep the mill just for spices, if possible, as you may find that the aromatic scent will flavour whatever else you grind later. Dried orange peel is very easy to make yourself. Use any peel from oranges you have eaten and dry it in a warm airing cupboard, or over a radiator or kitchen range.

½ measure dried thyme
½ measure dried rosemary
½ measure dried sweet woodruff
1 measure cinnamon sticks
1 measure dried orange peel
½ measure cloves
½ measure coriander seeds
¼ measure star anise
¼ measure powdered orris root

2 Grind small batches of the mixture at a time and empty the contents of the goblet into a large bowl after each grinding.

1 You will need to make small bags with fairly wide-necked openings to hold the finished mixture. Strip the leaves from the stems of the thyme and other herbs.

3 Stir the finished mixture well to distribute all the ingredients evenly. Scoop small amounts into the empty bags and then sew or tie them closed.

ABOVE: To scent a large cushion, place a small herb-filled sachet into a pocket sewn onto the cushion, which will impregnate the cushion with its scent.

Lavender Sachets

*T*hese are particularly attractive if made in a gauzy fabric such as muslin or silk organdie. Embroider a little heart on the front of the sachet and scallop the top edges, then overstitch these. You can use plain and simple lavender flowers on their own to fill the sachets, or mix in some orris root powder and perhaps some ground, dried lemon peel in the proportions 2 measures lavender to ¼ measure each of orris root powder and lemon peel, which will add a pungency to the scent.

Hop-filled Cushion

Hop

Hops have been the traditional sleeping herb for centuries. Their heady scent is supposed to make you feel relaxed and drowsy, so that you slide off to sleep quickly after a tense and tiring day. You can make the cushion from any fabric you choose but when it comes to filling it do this over some large sheets of paper, or outside, as the hops tend to fly around.

1 *Cut out two pieces of fabric into a square, put them right sides facing and carefully sew round three sides.*

2 *Turn them right way out and press the seams with an iron. Fill the cushion with loose, dried hops and then close the last side with small, neat hand stitches.*

Hop

3 *Finish with a ribbon wrapped once across the cushion, and decorate with a separate ribbon bow sewn neatly onto the centre of the cushion.*

Sweet Powder Mixture 2

*T*his is another version of the recipe on page 90. Don't bother to grind the cedarwood shavings if they are small, but simply add them to the other ground ingredients and mix them well.

1 measure red rose petals
½ measure lavender
½ measure rosemary
½ measure dried orange peel
¼ measure allspice
¼ measure cinnamon
¼ measure sugar
¼ measure powdered orris root
1 measure cedar wood shavings

Follow the method for Sweet Powder Mixture 1.

Herb Essential Oils

The many uses of plant essential oils are only now becoming widely understood as the interest in these substances grows. Aromatherapy using essential oils has made them more accessible to many people, who seem keenly interested to try out their other uses too. The oils are extracted from different parts of a plant, depending on the species used. Many oils come from the leaves or flowers of a plant but some come from the stems, fruits or roots. In some oils, the whole plant is used. Herb essential oils are generally derived from the leaves of the plant in question. They are the volatile oils which hold the aroma and the important properties which may be useful medicinally or for culinary purposes. Often, these essential oils are used in the cosmetic and perfume industries.

There are around 300 essential oils available today, produced from all around the world. They are extremely concentrated liquids and should always be handled carefully. Avoid allowing them to touch your skin undiluted; they are generally diluted in a carrying oil for massage. Store them in small, dark, glass bottles to keep them away from the light, which will cause them to deteriorate. Only a few drops are ever used at one time, either using an in-built dropper in the storage bottle or a separate pipette or eye-dropper.

Some herb essential oils can have very powerful properties. For example, thyme oil is twelve times more antiseptic than old-fashioned carbolic, and lavender oil has excellent healing properties when applied to burnt or damaged skin. A few people are sensitive to some herb oils such as thyme and cassia. Pure herb oils will vary in price according to the plant from which they derive. This is because some plants yield lots of oil and some very little. Some oils are also easier to extract than others. If a range of oils are all the same price, this is probably because they are not pure or have been diluted. Try to find a source of pure essential oils for the best results.

Bergamot

RIGHT: Essential oils are widely used nowadays, especially in aromatherapy, health massages and for making pot pourri. Herb oils vary in price depending on the herb from which they are derived.

Dried Oranges

*W*hole oranges or other citrus fruit can be carved, dried and used as decoration for a simple mixture of wood shavings. To carve the oranges you will need a special tool called a canelle knife which cuts a narrow groove into the peel. Once you have mastered its use, you can use it to cut stripes and patterns over the orange skin. You can stud the grooves with whole cloves if you wish. Keep any scraps and strips of peel and dry these to use in pot pourris and spice mixtures. Once you have cut the patterns in the skin, leave the oranges in a warm, dry, well-ventilated place to dry naturally. They will take several weeks to become completely dry and will shrink a little in the process. Uncut oranges will also dry, given time, but take longer than those which have been cut. Once they are dry, the oranges can be impregnated with drops of essential oil.

Wood Shaving, Chilli and Orange-scented Mixture

*I*f you wish to decorate this mixture with dried oranges, you will need to start preparing these well ahead of making the rest of the recipe. Natural wood shavings look best in this mixture, but dyed shavings are now available, and the subtler colours can be used effectively. Other fruits can be dried for use in scented mixtures – lemons, apple and peach slices. Choose the scent you like, but be sure it suits the style of mixture. A suitable mixture might be rosemary, orange and coriander. Display in an attractive container set on a low table to enjoy its scent and looks.

1 Using a canelle knife, carve decorative designs into the peel of several oranges, not only to make them attractive, but to speed up the drying process.

RIGHT: It is best to dry more oranges than you need, since one or two might rot or go soft before drying. But the fruit must be unwaxed or organically-produced to ensure the right results.

2 Once the oranges have dried, gather together the natural wood shavings, dried chillies, an essential oil of your choice and a shallow bowl to hold the mixture.

3 Place the wood shavings in the bowl, scatter the chillies on top, and then add the dried oranges. Put several drops of essential oil into the mixture, mixing it in thoroughly.

97

Scented Candles

Candle-making is not a mysterious science. In fact, it is quite easy to do once you have the correct ingredients and equipment. The most effective candles are simple to look at and poured rather than moulded. This means that you can pour the liquid wax into any suitable container which would hold a wick. Plain, thick, glass tumblers are ideal or use empty shells of all kinds. A mixture of plain, white candle wax and a small proportion of beeswax makes a candle with a nice, warm colour, pale cream rather than stark white. The crucial thing to remember with making candles is that the wick must be the right thickness for the diameter of candle. If it is not, the candle may not burn properly. Candle wick is sold in long lengths and will normally have instructions stating what size candle it is meant for.

1 *Choose the fragrance of oil you wish to add to the candle. It could be rose, jasmine, citrus, vanilla, bergamot (oswego or bee-balm), ylang-ylang, or citronella for* *outdoor candles. Candle wax comes in easy-to-melt granules these days. Make sure the shell is perfectly clean and will stand flat on a surface.*

Jasmine

2 *Put the wax and beeswax in a small saucepan and allow to melt over a very low heat. Be careful if you use gas, as wax is flammable. Dip a length of wick into the melted wax and leave to cool. This will make it stiff enough to put into the shell.*

3 *Attach the wick to the base of the shell with a small piece of plasticine. Support the top of the wick with a small, thin stick, such as a wooden skewer.*

4 *Add a few drops of essential oil to the melted wax, then pour it carefully into the shell. Leave to cool completely, then remove the stick and trim the wick to about 1cm/¹/₂ inch in length.*

Cedarwood Oil

Cedarwood essential oil can be used to impregnate small wooden shapes to be put inside drawers and cupboards. It is possible to buy the shapes already scented and they are often made from cedarwood themselves. Otherwise, any plywood or light wood shapes can be used, or some of the carved and moulded wooden objects designed to be used as scenters. The cedarwood fragrance can be topped up, when needed, by adding a few extra drops. Of course, you could use any fragrance you want but cedar is traditionally used for wardrobes and other furniture designed to hold clothes and fabrics. It has a lovely spicy, woody, resinous scent which is masculine and clean.

Cedarwood

1 Interesting leaf shapes can be easily cut from a light wood, such as balsa. Make templates from real leaves and draw around them onto the wood as a cutting guide.

2 To impregnate thoroughly the wooden shapes with the oil, place them in a plastic bag and sprinkle on the oil. Shake the bag and add more oil if you wish.

ABOVE: Try impregnating wooden shapes with allspice essential oil as a more pungent alternative to the more traditional cedar fragrance for scenting clothes.

Bergamot Oil

*B*ergamot essential oil has a fresh, citrusy floral scent, which blends well with rose geranium oil. Try combining it with a little bay essential oil, for a hint of sweet spice, and adding to a mixture of cape gooseberries (goldenberries or *Physalis peruviana*) and peach stones, garnished with nasturtium flowers.

RIGHT: Peach stones can be used to absorb fragrant essential oils in the same way as wooden shapes, and they add an interesting texture to mixtures.

Pot Pourri

*H*erbs of all kinds can be used to make a fabulous range of pot pourris. They don't have to be simply made in shades of green but can be as bright and colourful as you choose. Think of lavender, rose and marigold. Pot pourris should be subtle in scent and as attractive as possible. These days we tend to make dry mixtures of many different ingredients, which are not necessarily scented to start with, and then add the scent we require. This is fine, but it can sometimes produce some very garish and unattractive results. Using good, natural ingredients to start with will make a better pot pourri. If you grow herbs in your garden, then harvest some especially for making into pot pourris and pick flowers which are suitable for drying too, to add colour and different textures to the herb mix.

The basic principle for making a dry pot pourri is the same, whatever ingredients you use. Mix the perfectly dry petals, leaves, seed heads, flower heads and whatever you have chosen with ground or whole spices, other scented ingredients such as citrus peels and the all-important fixatives which will help the pot pourri to retain its scent. Then drops of essential oil are added to boost the perfume. This is where you can be quite creative and make your own special fragrances to suit your house and your taste. The most commonly used fixative is powdered orris root which is made from the rhizome of an iris grown in Italy. The powder looks like ground ginger and has a very faint perfume of violets. It has the ability though to 'fix' other scents and make them last longer. You may prefer to simply use an essential oil and keep topping it up when the fragrance fades. Orris root powder is available from herbalists' and florists'.

Lime blossom

RIGHT: *Once you have tried some of these recipes, experiment with your own combinations of different dried materials and scents, perhaps for different rooms in your home, or for special occasions or gifts.*

Some of the herbs suitable for pot pourris are thyme, rosemary, bay, sage, lemon verbena, sweet geranium, chamomile, lime (linden) blossom, savory, hyssop, marigold, rose, lavender and pineapple sage. It is possible to buy essential oils of many of these herbs and it is best to use the right oil for the herb you are using for a pot pourri, but you may like to combine herbs or add citrus oils or spice oils too.

Amounts have been given in volume, based on a standard measuring cup (250ml/8fl oz). You can increase or decrease the amounts to suit yourself.

Mixed Leaf and Herb Pot Pourri

*T*his makes a pretty soft green mixture which looks best displayed in a rustic earthenware bowl or a textured basket. The leaves you choose are not crucial; just try to get a good mix of large and small types.

1 cup dried eucalyptus leaves
1 cup dried bay leaves
1 cup lemon verbena leaves
½ cup uva-ursi (bearberry) leaves
½ cup dried thyme/rosemary/sage etc.
A few whole sprigs of dried thyme
½ cup powdered orris root
Several drops of lime (linden) flower, vervain
or rosemary essential oil

1 Put all the leaves into a large mixing bowl.

Eucalyptus

Red Rose Pot Pourri

A very simple mixture again, but one which always pleases. Using whole rosebuds makes a much more interesting mixture than petals. You can buy bags of loose rosebuds or buy the more expensive dried roses on stems and pick them off.

5 cups red or pink whole rosebuds
½ cup powdered orris root
¼ cup ground cloves
¼ cup ground allspice
4 drops oil of rose geranium
4 drops oil of ylang-ylang

Put the rosebuds into a large bowl and add the orris root and ground spices. Mix these very well together. Add the oils drop by drop, stirring the mixture all the time. Scoop it into paper bags and fold over the tops. Leave the bags in a cool dark place for at least four weeks to cure before displaying the pot pourri in small bowls or boxes.

2 Add the orris root and mix really well with your hands or a wooden spoon.

ABOVE: While keeping the overall subtle green colour scheme of this lovely pot pourri, use a range of variegated leaves to add interesting highlights.

3 Add several drops of oil, stirring as you do so. Put the mixture into large paper bags and loosely shut them with a dog-clip or clothes-peg. Leave in a cool, dark place to cure, preferably for several weeks before using them for display.

Marigold Pot Pourri

This is a lovely bright and sparkling pot pourri with the fresh and fruity scent of oranges and a hint of spice. Some whole spices, flower heads and slices of dried orange add greatly to the finished look of this pot pourri. Marigolds are simple to grow in the garden and they dry very easily, retaining their strong orange colour. The kind you need are pot marigolds (*Calendula officinalis*); some other varieties have an unpleasant smell.

4 cups dried marigold petals (or a mixture of yellow and orange flower petals, e.g. chamomile)
1 cup whole marigold flower heads
1 cup dried orange peel
½ cup small sticks of cinnamon
½ cup powdered orris root
¼ cup frankincense crystals
¼ cup ground cloves
¼ cup ground nutmeg
3 drops oil of bitter orange
3 drops oil of lemon
3 drops oil of cinnamon
Whole rings of dried orange to decorate

2 Add the peel, cinnamon, orris root, the frankincense (another fixative) and ground spices, and stir very thoroughly.

1 Put the dried flower heads and petals into a large bowl.

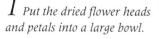

Marigold

3 Add the essential oils drop by drop, stirring the mixture as you do so. Put the mixture into paper bags, fold the tops over and secure lightly. Leave in a cool, dark place for at least four weeks to cure before displaying. Add the dried orange rings to the dish.

Lavender Pot Pourri

*T*his is often made from nothing more than plain lavender, but adding the fixative and oils will make it last longer. You can also add a little more colour by using some larkspur or cornflower heads. Decorate the finished bowl with a little tied bundle of lavender flower stems, simply finished with string or thread, or more elaborately tied with ribbon. Display this pot pourri in a wide, shallow bowl and make it in a fairly large quantity for the best effect. Dried lavender sold loose is usually not from the dark, purple-flowered varieties but if you grow your own lavender the colour choice for the pot pourri is yours depending upon which varieties you grow.

5 cups dried lavender
1 cup larkspur or cornflower heads or petals (optional)
½ cup powdered orris root
10 drops oil of lavender

Put the dried flowers into a large bowl. Add the orris root powder and mix very well. Add the oil drop by drop, stirring the mixture as you do so. Scoop the pot pourri into paper bags, turn over the tops and leave in a cool dark place to cure for about four weeks before displaying.

Fresh and Dried Posies

For as long as people have grown herbs and flowers, they have picked small bunches of them and made them into little posies in their hand. Posies make charming gifts and are the simplest and prettiest of any kind of flower arrangement. They also look pretty hanging from a ribbon to decorate a door, a wall or a piece of furniture. All through the year those with gardens can usually find enough herbs and flowers to pick and make a tiny, scented posy. Centuries ago, these little flower bunches had a more serious purpose than just to amuse or delight. 'Tussie-mussies', as they were called, were carried by the Great and the Good in an attempt to keep illness and infection at bay. High court judges carried a tussie-mussie with them, in the mistaken belief that smelling this fragrant posy would fend off disease such as the Plague. In those days, it was thought that a bad smell from drains or the street carried the illnesses and that a sweet scent would counteract this. The tradition lingers on to this day when the English monarch carries a posy on Maundy Thursday, when he or she distributes coins to the poor, in a ceremony dating back hundreds of years.

As well as fresh herb posies, it is possible to make dried ones too from a mixture of scented and non-scented materials. Any posy looks best if it is carefully thought out, with a good balance of colours and flower shapes, and perhaps a ring of leaves used as edging. Grey-leaved herbs look very pretty mixed in with other plants as they dry to a soft silvery colour. Examples are southernwood (field southernwood or artemisia), silver thyme, sage and lavender. Once you have bunched up the herbs and flowers into the right size of posy, tie the stems with string or fine wire and cut the base of the stems to a uniform length. Dried posies can have a little paper or lace collar, made from a doily, added to them for a Victorian look. Alternatively, bind the stems with a pretty ribbon finished off tied in a bow.

Hyssop

RIGHT: To create longer-lasting displays of fresh posies, place them in small glass vases – even attractively-shaped or decorated wine glasses – topped up with water.

To make the best dried posy, you should use ingredients which have already been dried, but you can also experiment with making small fresh posies which are then dried complete. Remember that these will shrink quite a bit as they dry and some of the herbs and flowers may dry at different rates. The effect will be very different from a posy made the first way, but the results are sometimes very pretty and unusual.

Bergamot

Fresh Herb Posy

A fresh herb posy made slightly larger than a tussie–mussie makes a very pretty flower arrangement to stand in a jug or any suitable container. This version has a red rose as the focal point and a lovely combination of other flowering herbs including hyssop, applemint, pink bergamot (oswego or bee-balm) and the starry blue flowers of borage. Begin with a single bloom, then build up the posy, adding rings of a different variety of flower around the central bloom. Here, the posy is edged with flowering hyssop. You can also make simpler versions, using just one type of flower such as the nasturtium posy.

BELOW: Traditionally, the outer ring of a posy or 'tussie-mussie' consists of a fragrant herb, so that the scent is released by the warmth of the hand that carries it. This posy is edged with minty hyssop.

Kitchen Herb Posies

If you grow plenty of herbs in the garden then some of the surplus can be dried for using in the winter. Even if you don't use all the leaves in cooking the bunches are pretty simply hanging as decorations. Always harvest herbs when they are dry and just before the middle of the day when their volatile oils, and therefore their scent, is at a maximum. Make small bunches and tie them tightly with wire. Make hooks from a length of thickish wire and hang the bunches by these hooks in a warm airy place. The ideal location is above a kitchen range which is permanently warm but a warm linen cupboard will do. Depending on the conditions, the bunches will take from five to ten days or so to dry completely. Suitable herbs for this air drying include rosemary, thyme, sage, hyssop, savory, southernwood, (field southernwood or artemisia) and marjoram.

Bouquet Garni Bunches

Traditional bouquet garni bunches make all the difference in flavour to soups, sauces and casseroles. Rather out of favour these days, they are nevertheless easy to put together if you have a fairly well-stocked herb garden. The classic bouquet garni contains a sprig of thyme, bay, curly-leaved parsley and sometimes a small piece of celery stem. You can adapt the herbs depending on the dish they are to flavour. Leave plenty of stalk on the parsley, as this is where all its flavour lies. You can also make bouquets garnis from dried herbs, but try always to use fresh parsley.

To make a collection of herb bouquets as a gift, gather fresh herbs together and once they are made up, keep them fresh in a shallow basket by covering the stem bases with clingfilm or tucking them into damp moss. You can also try freezing some for winter, packing them in clingfilm and then strong metal foil.

2 Combine a leaf or two of bay with a sprig of thyme and parsley for a classic combination and tie.

1 Sort out the different herbs and cut them into small manageable pieces. Cut some short lengths of string to have ready.

Thyme

3 If the bunches are to be gifts, label them with a suggestion about how to use them. This version is for a lamb casserole or for laying beneath a joint of roasting lamb. For pork, substitute sage for thyme, and push the mixture through a dried apple ring before tying. For beef, use the same combination as for lamb, but add a sprig of chervil and one of coriander.

Yellow Rose and Cinnamon Posy

*T*he finished posy is very pretty and sweet-smelling. Drops of essential oil, either lavender or cinnamon, can also be added, which will boost the fragrance further.

12 dried yellow roses
12 cinnamon sticks
12 carthamus (safflowers) flowers
12 echinops (or other thistles)
24 stems of lavender

Sort the various ingredients into separate piles. Start by putting one of each ingredient together into a bunch. Continue to do this, using twice as much lavender throughout the bunch. When you have a neat bunch and have used up all the flowers, tie the stems together tightly with wire and trim them off at the base.

Balls, Trees and Hearts

The decorative possibilities of dried herbs are really very great. They can be used in the same ways as dried flowers and in fact many herbs also fall into the dried flower category. Think of roses or lavender, for example. The advantage of many of the herbs is that they have their own natural fragrances which remain quite strong. Any of these decorations can have fragrance added too, by sprinkling a few drops of an essential oil over the dried materials. They will soak it up and release it gently, particularly when slightly warmed, near a lamp, for example.

Many of these more complicated decorations are very much more easily made using a hot-melt glue-gun rather than conventional glues and adhesives. Because glue from the gun sets firmly in such a short time, it speeds up jobs which would otherwise be very tedious, such as gluing individual leaves onto a preformed foam shape. The simplest glue-guns are not very expensive to buy and will rapidly pay for themselves. If you do not use one, then find an adhesive which holds and glues as quickly as possible and is suitable for use with natural materials.

Floral foam is suitable for cutting into various shapes and using as a base for herbal creations. The brown type sold for dried flowers is fine, but more expensive than the green sort sold for fresh flowers. The green is softer and easier to cut into shape, and it will be invisible if you completely cover it with plant materials. Use whichever you prefer or can get hold of easily.

Certain flowers, such as roses, are often sold stemless and loose in bags. It is cheaper to buy these than the dried roses complete with stems which, in any case, are a waste for these kinds of decorations. It is worth spending some time on the preparation of the materials for these decorations. Pick out a batch of matching flowers or leaves first and discard the rest to make the neatest and most symmetrical results.

Marjoram

RIGHT: *You can buy floral foam in a range of shapes nowadays, to use as bases for herb decorations. However, it is easy to cut your own shapes from foam block or board.*

Bay Leaf Tree

This is a variation on the more usual round or conical topiary tree. It uses dried bay leaves to cover a tall, rectangular foam shape. An old terracotta plant-pot is a sympathetic container, but you could use something else if you wish. You will need:

Piece of floral foam
10 straight twigs
About 100 bay leaves
1 terracotta plant-pot
Reindeer moss to cover the foam in the pot
Wire
Dried orange slices
Ribbon

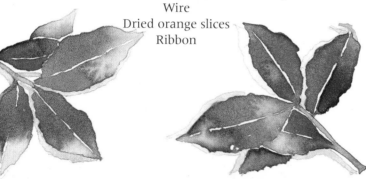

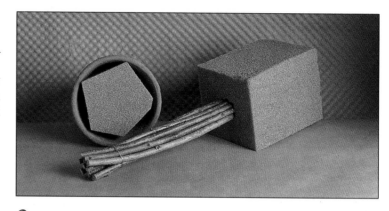

2 Push the twigs into the foam rectangle. Fill the pot with foam too and push the twigs stem down into this securely.

1 Cut the foam into a tall rectangle. Bind the twigs together into a bundle and wire them tightly at each end. Sort the bay leaves into piles of equal-sized leaves.

3 Start to glue the leaves neatly in place, snipping off any overlapping edges.

4 Completely cover the foam with leaves. Cover the foam in the pot with pieces of reindeer moss. Wire 2 slices of dried orange together, and attach them to a ribbon bow with wire. Push this wire into the foam in the pot.

Pink Rose Heart

Rose

*Y*ou will need a length of moss ribbon, which is available from craft shops or florists specialising in dried arrangements, and dried pink roses. Alternatively, make a heart from wire by pinching halfway along a piece (see Step 1), then bending back the ends to meet. Form a loop in one end and a hook in the other and attach. Bind moss onto the heart using fine reel wire.

Red Rose Ball

*T*his is very simple to make. You will need a foam sphere, of whatever size you choose, and plenty of rose heads. You will find that it takes a very large number of roses to cover the sphere. Glue them in place, working in a line round the circumference to begin with, then working in rows towards the top, and finally working downwards in the same way. Hold the ball gently as you glue, so as not to crush the flower heads. It may be easier to spear the ball on to a wooden skewer while you work. Tie a cord or ribbon around the finished sphere if you wish to hang it on a door or on a wall.

1 *Cut the moss ribbon to the length required to make a heart shape. Pinch it half-way along the length and dab it with a little glue. Bend the ribbon backwards on to itself until it is firmly glued.*

2 *Now bend the two ends back the other way, to make a point at the bottom. Glue the two ends together. You will find that a heart shape forms naturally.*

3 *Glue the roses right round the heart on the top edge of the ribbon. Attach a cord or ribbon if you wish to hang the finished heart.*

ABOVE: As a contrast in texture, colour and fragrance to these rose balls, you could coat small foam balls with glue and then roll them in dried lavender flowers.

Marjoram and Poppy Basket

*T*his idea relies on the heart-shaped container for its special effect but it would look equally pretty if made into a round or square basket. Again the glue-gun is necessary to fix the poppy seed-heads to the top edge of the basket. You will need:

Floral foam
1 small, heart-shaped basket
Enough dried poppy seed-heads to go
right round the top edge
Two bunches of dried marjoram flowers

Cut the foam to fit inside the basket and come a little below the level of the basket. Glue each poppy seed-head to the top edge of the basket, working in one direction only. Now take small bunches of the marjoram and push them into the foam to completely cover the whole basket. Aim to make a really dense mass of flowers so that no foam shows through. The marjoram should be lower than the poppy seed-heads.

Eucalyptus

LEFT: *The heart-shaped basket really makes this arrangement special – perfect as a centrepiece for a Valentine's Day celebration. Look out for interesting baskets to use.*

Eucalyptus Leaf Garland

*T*o make lengths of leaf garland all you need to do is:

1 Pick leaves off branches of fresh eucalyptus.

2 Thread them on to flexible wire. Hang them somewhere warm and airy and they will dry very quickly. Re-thread them on to string or wire again, this time closer together. You can also add other ingredients or different types of leaves between the eucalyptus. Try dried orange peel, dried flower heads or apple rings.

BELOW: *Make alternative garlands to this eucalyptus leaf example by combining herb leaves with other elements, for instance bay leaves and red chillies.*

Decorating
with Herbs

WREATHS AND GARLANDS
Pages 124-129

DECORATIVE HERB
BUNDLES
Pages 130-135

GARDEN POTS AND
CONTAINERS
Pages 136-143

INDOOR HERBS
Pages 144-151

WOODEN OUTDOOR
CONTAINERS
Pages 152-159

CHRISTMAS HERB
DECORATIONS
Pages 160-167

Wreaths and Garlands

Wreaths and garlands of flowers and foliage have become very popular over the last few years. Garlands made from dried material, in particular, make wonderfully decorative additions to the house, where they can be hung formally on a door or wall or hooked more casually across the corner of a bedhead, mirror or piece of furniture. Some kinds are very quick to make and require only small amounts of ingredients, so they are excellent for decorations which are needed in a hurry when something a little more festive and special than an ordinary arrangement is the order of the day.

Herbs, both fresh and dried, make marvellous ingredients for wreaths. Their scent is, of course, an added bonus to the finished item, and many of the flowering herbs are very pretty in their own right as cut flowers. You have a choice of how to construct your wreath. There are many ready-made wreath bases available. These are usually made from twigs or vine-stems twisted into a ring. They are good-looking enough to use on their own but they can also be used as a base to which other plant material can be attached. This is done by gluing dried stems to the twigs or wiring in fresh stems or even by just pushing flowers and foliage in amongst the twigs. Then there are simple foam rings designed for dried flowers to be either glued or pushed into place. There are also foam rings with a plastic backing which can be soaked in water and used for fresh flowers and herbs. These are easy to use and give a very professional effect, though you do need plenty of material to cover the base, as they must be closely packed with flowers to prevent any foam from showing through.

Many different herbs are suitable for using to make wreaths and garlands, including lavender, roses, sage, thyme, rosemary, bay, and many of the shrubbier kinds of herbs with woody stems.

Lavender

RIGHT: Herb-decorated wreaths and garlands make such versatile decorations – as simple and spontaneous as a few bunches of herbs tucked into a twig ring, or as elegant as a wreath of fresh, full-blown roses and summer-flowering herbs for a special occasion.

Rose and Golden Marjoram Garland

*T*his is a fresh flower-and-herb garland built up on a moist floral foam wreath base. Make sure that the foam is thoroughly wetted before inserting the flowers, though it should not be saturated. Check any instructions that may have come with it for the exact length of soaking time, since these may vary. Work outdoors or on a waterproof surface because as you push the stems into place, the foam usually drips quite a lot. This garland is intended for making when roses are plentiful in early summer. The varieties used here are two vibrant cerise pink ones, Charles de Mills and *Rosa gallica officinalis* or the Apothecary's Rose.

Golden marjoram is a highly decorative garden plant. The leaves that emerge in spfing are a bright lime-green colour and if grown in a partly-shaded place, this fresh colour is maintained all summer, or it may fade slightly to a less bright but still golden green. It makes a lovely contrast with many other colours.

1 Soak the foam ring ready for use and collect all the plant material. The items used here are golden marjoram, deep pink roses, rosemary and lavender, with some small-leaved evergreen leaves as a filler.

2 Cut all the plant stems short and start to make the garland by putting marjoram, sprigs of rosemary and the evergreen leaves all over the foam, working round it systematically until the whole ring is well-covered. Now add the roses and lavender, spacing them evenly throughout the foliage.

ABOVE: *Attach a loop of wire or string if you wish, from which to hang the wreath when it is finished. It will keep fresh for several days, especially if it is sprayed occasionally with water from a plant-mister.*

Golden marjoram

Dried Roses on Willow Wreath

Create a small bunch of dried roses and wire them together. Cut the rose stems very short. Wire them to a pale willow wreath and attach a bow made from wide, wire-edged ribbon beside the roses, to create a decorative effect.

RIGHT: *A flamboyant ribbon adds the finishing touch to this pretty wreath. Wire-edged ribbon is wonderful to use in floral decorations, since it can be moulded into soft, flowing shapes.*

127

Lavender Wreath

This pretty and informal wreath makes use of a ready-made vine twig ring and several different varieties of lavender. As the lavender stems are not kept moist in any way, they will slowly wilt and then dry out naturally. However, the wreath will look pretty for a special occasion and could subsequently be air-dried to keep for use as a dried decoration.

If you have a vine growing in your garden, it is possible to make your own wreaths. The vine should be harvested as the leaves drop in autumn but while the stems are still pliable. They can then be cut, and long lengths twisted round and round and the loose ends tucked under each other. You may need to hold the stems together in places with a little thin wire, discreetly placed so as to make it invisible. Make the ring round a cylindrical shape of some kind so that you get a perfect circle. Leave the vine ring to dry out naturally, and then decorate it how you like, with dried or fresh material of your choice.

1 *Collect several different types and colours of fresh lavender, ensuring that the flower heads have stems that are as long as possible.*

2 *Work round the garland in one direction, tucking little bunches of two or three stems of lavender at a time under the vine twigs. Lavender stems are quite bendable and will generally thread fairly easily. If you have problems, then tie them in with small pieces of thin wire.*

3 *Continue round the garland, adding lavender bunches and varying the colours as you go. Do not aim to cover the twigs completely with flowers. Finish off with a little bow of narrow purple ribbon and a loop from which to hang the wreath.*

Feverfew

Fresh Herb Bunch on a Twig Ring

*T*his makes the most of the decorative qualities of the ring itself which just has a tiny bunch of fresh herbs added to it. The finished ring could be hung or would look lovely as a table decoration for a summer meal outdoors.

You can make a small posy from whatever herbs you have to hand which are pretty and decorative. As previously suggested, the posy could later be hung in a warm, dry place to air-dry. The herbs could then be used in cooking or pot pourris, depending on the particular herbs used.

Lavender

1 *Gather together all the herbs you want to use. Shown here are feverfew, golden marjoram, santolina, and lavender.*

2 *Tie the stems of the herbs with a small length of raffia or coloured twine, and then attach these to the ring at an angle.*

Decorative Herb Bundles

It is a traditional sight in summer wherever scented herbs are grown to see bunches of them, such as lavender, harvested and hung up to dry. They are dried in this way because it is practical and easy, but of course it also happens to be very decorative. Using this functional idea as a starting point, all kinds of pretty and unusual versions of a tied bundle can be made from fresh or dried herbs. You can make bundles which stand upright like small corn stooks to create an unusual display, if you make them thick enough at the base to support themselves without any help, or tie bunches of a single type of herb or pretty mixtures of different herbs, to hang singly or in groups.

Bundles made from fresh herbs should be stood in water to make them last more than a few hours, or they can be hung in the fresh air to dry just as they are. Bundles made from dried herbs are generally simple to create, needing only patience to organise the stems and get them to equal lengths, with the flowers or leaves in a neat arrangement above them. Bundles can be further decorated with ribbons, bows, coarse string, natural or coloured raffia or anything else that takes your fancy. You can add other ingredients such as cinnamon sticks or little bunches of dried fruits or decorative spices. Whether fresh or dry, the plants you use will need to have straight, stiff stems to stand on their own unless you are going to bind them very tightly with something which will add strength, in which case you can then use materials with weaker stems.

RIGHT: These decorative bunches offer a creative way of displaying all kinds of herbs. Try placing a fragrant bundle in a hallway, where the scent will be able to circulate.

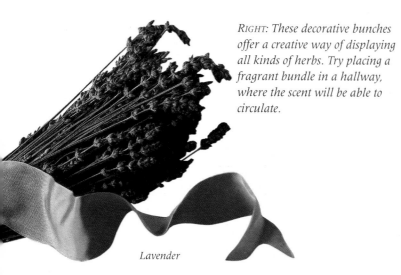

Lavender

Use the finished bundles as decorations anywhere in the house. A pair of dried herb stooks would look elegant at either end of a mantelshelf or flanking a pretty ornament or picture frame. A single bundle can be tucked in amongst cherished possessions on a shelf or low table, and scented versions are lovely on a dressing table or bedside table. Some bundles are more suitable for a kitchen dresser or shelves, particularly if they are made from the culinary herbs such as bay, rosemary, sage or thyme.

Dried Lavender Bundle

*D*ried lavender is available in small bunches from dried flower suppliers and flower shops. The type sold is usually a dark purple-flowered type, often from a dwarf variety, and hence the stems are never very long. This doesn't normally matter but try to get the longest stems possible otherwise you may end up discarding some which are too short. The length of stem is important to the overall proportions of the finished bundle and the bare stems should ideally be about one-and-a-half times to twice the length of the flowered part.

1 You will need several small bunches of lavender to make one bundle. You will also need wire or string for tying and mauve wire-edged ribbon.

Lavender

2 Unwrap the lavender bunches and discard any stems which are too short or damaged.

3 Begin to re-make a bunch, keeping the flower heads together and at the same level. Don't worry about the stems so much at this stage.

4 When you have made a bunch large enough, tie it tightly. Now trim the stems so that they are perfectly even and the bundle will stand on its own. Finish off with the wire-edged ribbon.

Cinnamon and Rose Stook

*T*his is another dried bundle in a slightly different style. It makes use of deliciously-scented cinnamon sticks to make the base, as rose stems are thin and often not very straight. You could add extra scent to the bundle by sprinkling some essential oils on to the flowers and seed-heads. A pair of these stooks would look lovely in winter as a mantelshelf decoration. The ribbon you choose can change the look of the bundle completely. A red-and-gold one like the one used here looks traditional and even festive, while a plain red or ginger-coloured ribbon would look more everyday in style. You will need about:

12 small poppy seed-heads
Thin wire
25 small dried red roses
12 sticks of cinnamon, all the same length
Ribbon

1 Gather together all the materials you need before you begin. Make a small bunch of the seed-heads to form the centre of the bundle. Tie the stems securely with thin wire.

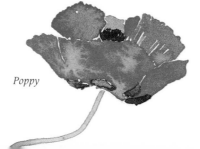

Poppy

ABOVE: A very elegant dried bundle, this cinnamon and rose stook would make a memorable gift for a special friend.

134

2 *Add roses around the poppies, framing them neatly, and wire the stems again to hold everything tight. Cut the stems shorter than the cinnamon sticks.*

3 *Put the cinnamon sticks around the stems with the tops quite high up under the flowers. Tie these tightly with wire. Cover the wire with a pretty bow.*

Rosemary, Marjoram and Thyme Bundle

*T*his bundle is made in a slightly different way as it is designed to be seen from the front so that the three herbs are layered one above the other. Of course, it is quite difficult to make natural plants perfectly symmetrical but try with this to make it as neat and organised as the herbs will allow. You will need a small bunch of straight-stemmed rosemary, flowering marjoram and shrubby thyme (not the creeping type which would be too short). Lay the marjoram on the rosemary, leaving the rosemary to show about 5cm/2in above the flowers. Now put the thyme under the marjoram. Tie all the stems together, then trim them off to the same length all over so that they stand on their own. Wrap a narrow leaf, such as an iris leaf, around the wire or string used to tie the stems, to conceal it, or try using grass, green tissue or natural green raffia for binding.

Garden Pots and Containers

Perhaps the best way to grow herbs in a garden is in pots and containers of all kinds. It means that even the smallest town courtyard can have at least a few leaves of something delicious for the kitchen or a decorative mixture of herbs to look at. It is possible to appreciate all the wonderful textures and shapes of herb foliage and the colours and scents of the plants when they are grown in this way. Bringing them up above ground level, too, means that you are tempted to pinch a leaf or release the scent as you brush near the leaves.

It is important when mixing herbs together in one container that you choose compatible plants, unless you are only aiming for a short-term display. Shrubby herbs such as thyme which love good drainage and love the sunlight might not be too happy combined with a water-loving mint. In the main, though, most herbs are quite easy to cultivate and will survive together because they are basically easy and good-natured plants. Take care not to plant very large herbs such as lovage or angelica in a small container which they might quickly outgrow. On the other hand, though, a container can be a good way of keeping a rampant herb in check. Mints, for example, are notorious spreaders in the garden, taking over wherever they are planted, but grown in a container their roots are safe from causing harm to other smaller plants.

Terracotta and ceramic pots always look good planted with herbs and they are long-lasting and age well providing that they are frostproof. Plastic never looks so good, but it can mean you spend less time watering plants in the summer because the soil in them will not dry out as fast as that in porous containers. If you use terracotta pots then it is best to use heavier soils and composts rather than soil-free types which can dry out very fast and are difficult to re-hydrate.

Sage

RIGHT: A glorious grouping of herb-planted pots and containers offers so many good things – an attractive outdoor display, wonderful scents and a ready source of natural flavourings and garnishes for use in the kitchen.

Some herbs, such as the more tender rosemary, lavender and lemon verbena, will need to be brought into a frost-free environment during the winter, so they can be planted in decorative pots with no fear of winter causing the containers damage.

Containers can be planted with colour in mind, or for culinary purposes. They may be a collection of plants which need similar conditions or just a lovely mixture of scents. Another big advantage to planting herbs in pots is that they can be moved around the garden or grouped with other containers to make an ever-changing display. The four ideas here are designed first and foremost to look good, concentrating on interesting mixtures of leaf colour and shape.

Thyme with Pebbles

*T*hyme loves the sun and good drainage and the various varieties are very happy growing between paving stones. Re-create these conditions in a pot with a covering of fine pebbles over the surface of the soil. This planting uses a shallower pot as the plants are not very deep-rooting. Use an upright thyme such as this silver variegated variety, or choose a creeping kind and then use finer grit as the soil covering.

1 Choose a pretty pot for this display. Put a shallow layer of pebbles or grit at the base of the pot for drainage. Fill the pot almost to the top with a good gritty compost or rich soil.

2 Plant one or two thyme plants depending on their size.

Thyme

3 Scatter a layer of small pebbles over the surface, being careful not to damage the plants, which will eventually grow and spread out to fill the pot.

RIGHT: *Sage provides a good contrast in leaf size and shape to the small-leaved thyme. Here, variegated varieties of both herbs are combined to great effect.*

Mediterranean Mixture

This is a combination of herbs which is especially good for a sunny site. Combine French lavender with dwarf English lavender and purple-flowered heliotrope (*Heliotropium peruviana*, sometimes called cherry pie because of its scent). Use a well-drained soil or compost and, at the end of the summer, move the pot into a greenhouse or shelter it from frost in some other way. Replace the heliotrope each year, or try using other herbs combined with the lavenders.

LEFT: *Lavender is a herb of Mediterranean origins and the fields of lavender found in the south of France are a breathtaking sight. There are many different varieties of lavender to choose from.*

ABOVE: *Another herb planting featuring the striking French lavender, superbly set off by the blue hue of the container – a demonstration of what a difference your choice of pot can make.*

Bronze and Purple Herb Pot

*U*se a fairly heavy, soil-based compost, mixed with a lighter soil-free compost rather than a purely peat-based one, which will be too light and dry out very quickly. For this mixture you will need:

A pale-mauve, glazed ceramic container
2 purple basil
2 bronze fennel
1 purple-and-cream variegated sage
Potting compost
Gravel for drainage

1 Lay down a layer of gravel or something similar to provide some free drainage for the pot.

2 Add the compost about three-quarters of the way up the pot.

RIGHT: A mixed planting of herbs with colourful foliage makes an effective contrast to combinations of flowering herbs in neighbouring pots. Look out for unusual herb varieties at nurseries.

3 Plant the taller bronze fennels at the back, then add the basils and finally the sage. Basils are annual plants and will need to be replaced each year, while the fennel and sage are perennial. Fennel produces bright yellow flowers from midsummer, which will bring additional colour and interest to the planting well into autumn.

Pineapple mint

Lemon balm

ABOVE: Lemon balm both tastes and smells of lemon. It's a good choice for wildlife enthusiasts, since its aromatic scent attracts bees. The plant bears pale yellow or white flowers in the summer.

RIGHT: Even if you have a ground-planted herb garden, an attractive pot of herbs can make an impressive focal point within the garden, especially planted with golden-leaved herbs.

142

Golden-leaved Herbs in a Container

*T*his mixture will keep its fresh leaf colour through the summer. Stand it out of very hot sun as this will help to keep the colours fresh. Golden-leaved herbs prefer shade or semi-shade best. For this planting you will need:

1 tall ceramic pot in a greenish-brown glaze
2 golden lemon balm plants
1 lemon-flowered santolina
1 cream variegated sage

Lemon balm

1 *Put a layer of grit, pebbles or some pieces of broken terracotta pot in the base of the container to aid drainage.*

2 *Fill with good soil or compost.*

3 *Plant the two balms at the back, the santolina to one side and the sage on the other. Fill with more soil if necessary. Water well.*

143

Indoor Herbs

Many people have no garden or have no desire to do any outdoor gardening. Herbs can provide perfect plants for indoor gardening and are especially good for this purpose as they can be both useful and decorative. Many supermarkets these days sell little growing pots of herbs to snip and use in cooking and as they are growing they remain fresh for as long as you need them. They are not generally suitable for planting into your own containers, though, and growing on for longer periods. For this purpose, you can raise your own plants from seed. Many herbs are easy to cultivate in this way, but for indoor gardening, where conditions are never absolutely perfect, it is probably better to start off with good, well-grown young herb plants, which you can buy from a nursery or garden centre.

Most herbs will require plenty of light and moisture. Do not attempt to grow herbs if you cannot provide natural light for most of the day. They can be placed in or near a window as long as they won't get too much direct sunlight at the hottest times of the day during the summer. But even winter sun can occasionally be damaging to tender plants. A very dry atmosphere is not good for many plants, though some, such as sweet geraniums, are not bothered by these conditions. The chances are that your indoor herb garden will end up in the kitchen and this is probably the most suitable place for it.

Take care and trouble in choosing or decorating special containers or devise ways to display herbs more unconventionally than in a row on the windowsill. Try hanging pots from wires, or planting herbs in hanging baskets or fixing glass shelves across a window which is not often opened. Keep plants moist but not overwatered and if possible use rainwater rather than tap water, to which plants may react badly if it is used exclusively.

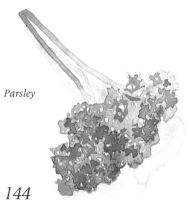

Parsley

RIGHT: It is easy and rewarding to create a herb display indoors, but like most plants, herbs need a certain amount of attention to keep them in good condition.

Feed healthy, growing indoor herbs with liquid fertiliser every week during the summer months. Don't be afraid to trim them often and pinch out growing tips to encourage them to bush out, since herbs grown indoors can get a little tall and stringy. Certain plants, such as basil and geranium, positively thrive on being trimmed regularly. It is important to keep basil from flowering so that it will continue to produce plenty of new leaves. Once it has been allowed to flower it will give up, thinking it has done what it should.

If you do have a garden but still like to grow herbs indoors, you can give plants the occasional holiday outside during the summer. This will boost their growth and health. They can then be brought back in again when the weather turns cooler.

Curly-leaved parsley

Hanging Wire Pot-holder

*F*or this idea you will need some green plastic-coated wire which is strong, but flexible enough to bend with pliers quite easily. Once you have tried to make one of these you can experiment with different variations on the same theme.

1 Decide on the pot and plant you are going to make the hanger for as it should be made to fit. Have some wire-cutters and pliers ready, and the roll of green wire.

2 Make a circle of wire to fit round the top of the pot, just below the ledge. Make three loops by twisting the wire in three places equally spaced around the ring.

Join the ends by twisting the wires together. Cut three lengths of wire to make the hangers and a shorter piece for the top loop.

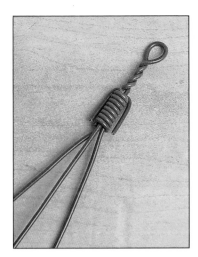

3 Attach the three straight pieces
of wire to each loop in the ring and
bring them together at the top.

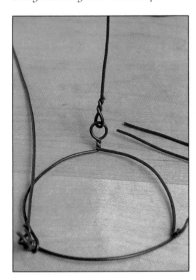

4 Twist them together and make a
loop with the smaller piece of wire,
twisting it into a neat spiral. Drop
the pot into the ring and hang it
from another piece of wire threaded
through the top loop.

RIGHT: *The ever-popular, curly-
leaved parsley is treated to a rather
more creative method of display
than in a pot on a windowsill. The
pot-holder is simple to make and
natural in its effect.*

Basils in a Basket

*B*asil plants seem to thrive indoors as they need high temperatures and a sheltered site to do well, so the kitchen window is ideal if the sunlight is indirect. They also respond well to feeding with a liquid fertiliser and plenty of moisture to keep them growing fast and producing lots of lush leaves. Pick out any flower buds to induce greater leaf production.

Purple basil

2 Cut a piece of black plastic the same shape as the base of the basket but a little larger all round. Put it into the bottom of the basket.

1 You will need a basket which is narrow enough to sit on a windowsill, black plastic to line it and three or more basil plants. Mix purple with green for a more interesting effect.

3 Now simply stand the basil plants close together inside the basket and put the basket in a well-lighted window.

Basil

149

Pigment-coloured Pots

*P*lain, new, terracotta pots can be made to look far more interesting by colouring them with paint pigment. There are several ways to do this. Where you wish to use the pots once they are coloured will determine the materials you use. You can mix the powdered pigment with linseed oil and paint this mixture on to the pot. The oil soaks into the terracotta and absorbs some of the colour. The rest of the pigment stays on the surface and looks very natural, like the normal matt texture of clay. The pigment will wear away slightly with weathering and handling, leaving a lovely surface finish. On indoor pots, this may be a problem so it is better for pots being used exclusively indoors to mix the powdered pigment with a matt PVA paint medium well thinned down with water.

1 Mix red and ochre pigments with a little water and PVA paint medium to create a warm red shade.

2 Paint it over the outside of the pot with a broad sponge.

3 Leave the pot to dry outdoors before planting it. A scented geranium with deep-red flowers is the perfect choice for the painted pot.

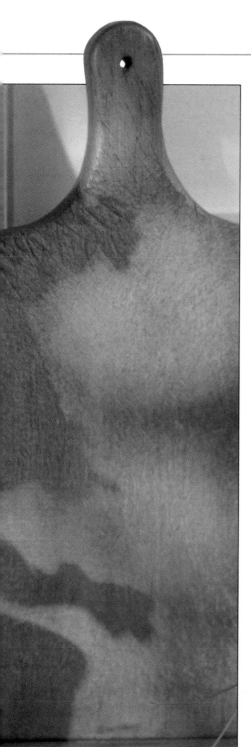

A Painted Trio of Pots

Chives

Pigment-painted pots in blue, yellow and green are used here to contain healthy chives, helxine and curly-leaved parsley.

LEFT: *The red of this simply-painted, terracotta pot echoes the colour of the geranium's flowers, while providing a dramatic contrast to the blue tablecloth.*

ABOVE: *A simple grouping of these brightly-coloured, pigment-painted pots makes an eye-catching display. Snip off the chive flowers to retain the herb's flavour.*

Wooden Outdoor Containers

Containers for outdoor plantings have been made from wood for as long as people have been gardening. Alongside stone and clay, wood has always been a very important material in garden construction and decoration. Where once woods such as oak and elm would have been used, nowadays soft woods have generally taken their place, especially as people have moved away from the ecologically-unsound imported tropical woods such as teak. Soft woods will never last as long as hardwoods but these days they are treated with preservatives and stand up to reasonable wear and tear in the garden. They can be painted easily or stained with wood dyes and it doesn't seem a shame to cover up plain old pine whereas oak, for example, ages and weathers to a lovely silver-grey outside and it almost seems like sacrilege to cover it.

There are many special paints designed for outdoor use and specifically for wood, so look out for them; they come in a good variety of colours. It is fun to match the colour of your container with the plants inside or to choose contrasting or even clashing colours, depending how bold you feel and the effect you are after. There is nothing to stop you changing the colour of your wooden window boxes every year if you want to. Many paints can be used straight over new or old wood without preparation, primers or undercoats and are meant to be micro-porous to let the timber 'breathe'.

LEFT: Weathered wooden tubs, such as this example, have a charm all of their own and really don't need any dressing up.

RIGHT: Look out for any discarded wooden crates or boxes that would make interesting containers for your herbs, especially when enhanced with colourful paints.

Marjoram

Search out wooden containers which can be recycled from their former use to make attractive planters for herbs. Even if they are short-term, lasting perhaps only for one season, something like a cheap wooden oyster crate will still look good with plants growing in it rather than throw it away. Fruit and vegetables are still packed in wooden trays which can be painted and used as plant containers for small and shallow-rooted herbs, such as varieties of thyme. Use your initiative and try anything which could conceivably be adapted easily to hold plants. An empty wooden whisky or sherry barrel, cut in half, is still one of the best of all containers for displaying plants and is large enough to accommodate quite a good-sized and well-established herb garden for many years. In this case, it is definitely more handsome if it is left in its natural wood colour.

A Collection of Thymes in a Fruit Box

ABOVE: Common thyme is the culinary variety and a cultivated form of the wild thyme which grows in the mountainous regions of Mediterranean countries.

RIGHT: Different varieties of thyme have varying colours of flowers, from white to crimson, as well as foliage of different hues, including bright green and blue-grey.

*T*his planting uses an ordinary thin wooden fruit box painted a pretty, soft green to complement the thyme plants inside. When it is planted and the herbs are growing, it would look prettiest put somewhere above the ground, on a table or pedestal of some kind. Thymes like sunlight and good drainage. You will need a wooden fruit box, plastic to line it, suitable matt paint, soil and thyme plants.

Thyme

1 Use a special exterior or wood paint in a matt finish, in a shade of green, to paint the outside of the box and a little way down the inside edges. Leave to dry.

2 Line the base and slightly up the inside edges with a rectangle of black plastic. Puncture tiny holes all over the plastic to allow for drainage.

3 Fill the box with soil that has had some grit added to it then plant it with as many small thyme plants as will fit inside. Put the taller ones at the back and the lower-growing ones at the front of the box.

Oyster Box with Scented Pelargoniums

*P*elargoniums are commonly called geraniums and there is often confusion over the two names. Scented pelargoniums are lovely plants to grow in a greenhouse or garden, and each variety has a different scent in its foliage. Many of them have quite insignificant flowers and are mainly grown for their foliage. For a collection like this one it is good to add a few more showy types of pelargoniums such as the Uniques or Regals to add some colourful flowers to the display. Line the oyster box with plastic and fill with good gritty soil or compost. Plant a mixture of pelargoniums and perhaps a lavender or rosemary plant to give a contrast of foliage. Keep this box in a sunny position and water sparingly but regularly.

LEFT: Different varieties of scented pelargoniums offer a range of wonderful scents, from the fruity fragrances of apple and orange, to rose-lemon or peppermint.

ABOVE: This wooden barrel makes an attractive container for herbs and hostas. Line with plastic that has been pierced to create holes for drainage.

Viola Trug Basket

A pretty display for spring and early summer made using purple violas planted in a small wooden trug. You could use any decorative shallow, woven basket instead of a trug. Once the violas have finished flowering in late summer you could take out the plants and plant them into a border to flower the following year. While the plants are in flower the basket would look very pretty as a focal point on a garden table.

1 Drill small holes in the trug for drainage and treat the wood with a preservative to prevent it from rotting.

2 Then simply fill it with soil over a layer of drainage material.

3 Plant it with several small viola plants as if it were a conventional container. Water them well and top up with more soil if necessary.

Viola

Chives

BELOW: *A plain window box sets off a lush mixture of herbs, including thyme, parsley, chives, violas and nasturtiums.*

Mixed Herbs in a Window box

A window box planted with herbs makes a very successful display as it is possible to use plants that look good all year round. With a basis of perennial herbs permanently planted you could then add other annual varieties or flowers to bring colour and in the spring you could have small bulbs coming up and flowering through and between the plants which are already there. A soft blue paint colour is a very sympathetic choice to complement the herbs inside. Use a matt paint for the most subtle finish. The window box below contains buckler-shaped sorrel (French sorrel, *Rumex scutatus*), golden thymes, variegated sage and marjoram.

French sorrel

RIGHT: *Here, sage, lavender and scented geraniums are cleverly combined with strawberry plants for a really luscious display.*

BELOW: *Ideally, French sorrel should be grown in full sun, in a rich, well-drained soil.*

Christmas Herb Decorations

Christmas might not be connected with herbs in most peoples' minds as we tend to think of summer as being the season of herbs and their scents and flavours. Yet quite a few herbs are still green and fragrant through the winter months and many are decorative in their dried state. The glossy leaves of box and bay are in fine condition to make into decorations and rosemary is often in flower through milder spells of winter weather. Thymes are evergreen too though they may not be as pungent in scent during the winter months as they are in the summer.

Natural decorations at Christmas are always prettier than artificial ones and if you are well-prepared you can have all kinds of lovely ingredients to use. Collect leaves in the autumn and press them flat and dry, and pick berries to store on the stem or allow them to dry naturally. Dried roses and other summer flowers can add any colour you may need and silver-and-white dried flowers and foliage bring a touch of glitter and frost. Combine these with spices and other scented items, such as dried and fresh citrus peels, eucalyptus leaves, nuts in their shells, popcorn, seed-heads and fruits. If you want to make everything look a little more glamorous, then you can add touches of silver and gold with paint, spray or gold and silver leaf. Keep this to a minimum though or it will threaten to overpower the subtle prettiness of the natural elements.

The most effective kinds of decorations are often the simplest in concept, so don't try to make anything which is too complicated or contrived. Tiny bunches of dried flowers and herbs make charming Christmas tree decorations, either wired into place or tied with thin gold cord or ribbon to the branches. A tree completely covered in these little posies would look quite spectacular, or they could be used in amongst other more conventional decorations.

RIGHT: Bring the magic of herbs to your festive decorations this year. Rosemary (the symbol of friendship), with its pungent, piney smell, makes a delightful substitute for the more predictable Christmas greenery.

Thyme

160

Table settings for the Christmas festivities can benefit from the herb treatment too. A simple pyramid of fresh fruits, shiny red apples, lemons or oranges, looks magnificent when spiked with sprays of glossy bay leaves. Or tiny bunches of fresh herbs can be tied onto a napkin for each guest. Dried red roses and fresh rosemary would make beautiful posies to decorate each place setting, especially if they were standing in small red glasses. The possibilities are endless, once the imagination gets going, so do consider using herbs both fresh and dried for the next festive season.

Pomegranate Pyramid

*P*omegranates are wonderfully festive, with their spectacular rich red and coral colouring, and pretty shapes. Nothing could be simpler than making a pile of these fruits and contrasting them with a few pieces of evergreen herb, to create an arresting centrepiece for an extra-special Christmas lunch or dinner. After you have finished the decoration leave the pomegranates in a warm airy place to dry naturally. They can then be used for other decorations at a later date. You will need:

Glass-stemmed dish or comport
8 pomegranates
Small red apples and/or berries
Bunch of fresh bay
Bunch of fresh rosemary

2 First pile the pomegranates on to the dish. Arrange the apples and berries in between.

Rosemary

1 Gather your ingredients together. Polish the fruits with a soft cloth.

3 Cut single leaves of bay and push them between the fruits. Do the same with sprigs of rosemary.

Tree Decorations

Small bunches to tie to the tree are quick and easy to make and, if stored carefully, can be used year after year. If the rosemary is fresh, it will dry naturally while it is on the tree. Add a few drops of essential oil to the decorations if you wish. You will need:

Fresh or dried rosemary
Dried gypsophila (baby's breath)
Small red dried roses
Dried cornflowers
Thin wire

2 Lay two or three sprigs of rosemary on the working surface. Add a sprig of gypsophila (baby's breath).

3 Add a few roses and cornflowers to make a neat spray.

1 Gather all the ingredients together. Cut the lavender and gypsophila (baby's breath) into small sprigs, and place in separate piles for easy access. Trim the rose stems.

4 Tie the stems together with wire to make a little fan-shaped spray of flowers. Leave a length of wire long enough to attach the spray to the Christmas tree.

Herb-decorated Candles

*I*t is lovely to light the house with plenty of candlelight at Christmastime. Use large, slow-burning church candles and attach small bunches or sprigs of herbs to each. Tie with a richly-coloured festive ribbon. Never leave a lighted candle unattended in case it burns down too quickly.

ABOVE: These pretty little sprays of flowers and herbs could also be used to decorate mirrors or picture frames, or napkins for a festive table setting.

RIGHT: A collection of candles of varying sizes, similarly adorned with bunches of herbs, would make an atmospheric and aromatic table centrepiece for a festive feast.

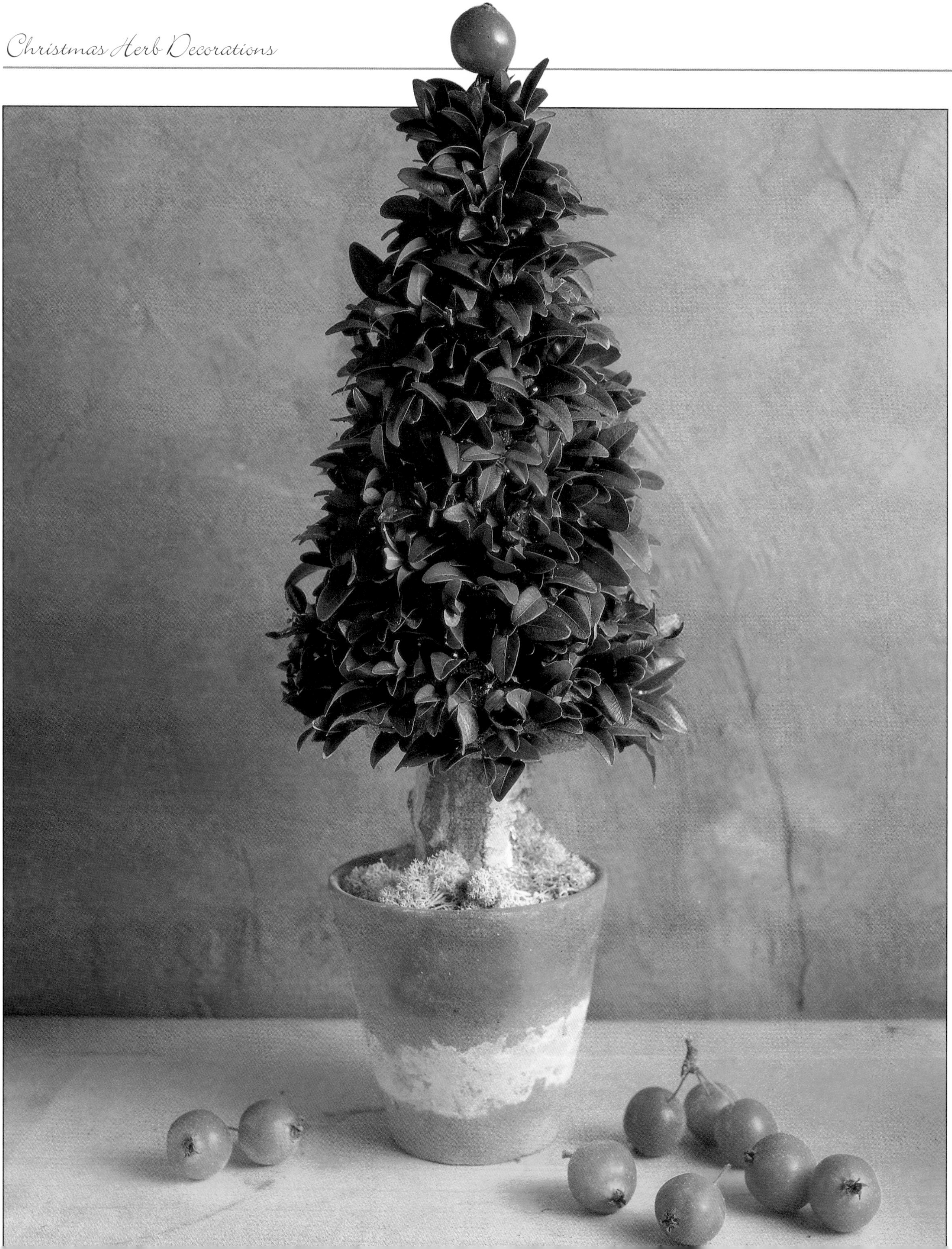

Conical Boxtree

This little tree can be made any size you like. If it is hard to find box, use any other fresh or dried small-leaved evergreen foliage, even a mixture of different kinds for a variation in texture and tone. If you prefer, the tree foliage can simply stand straight on a surface, without a stem in a pot. You will need:

Box branches
Glue-gun
Cone-shaped floral foam
Short length of branch for tree trunk
Terracotta pot
Floral foam to fill the pot
Reindeer moss

2 Working from the base of the cone, glue the sprigs of box to the foam, working round systematically and aiming to completely cover the foam.

1 Cut the box branches into small, manageable sprigs. Heat up the glue-gun.

Box

3 When the cone is covered with leaves, cut a small hole from the base to fit the trunk. Glue the trunk to the base. Fill the pot with foam and push the trunk into place. Decorate with real or artificial fruit and perhaps place a bauble on the top of the tree. Cover the foam in the pot with small pieces of reindeer moss.

Herbs for Health and Beauty

BATH OILS, SCRUBS
AND GELS
Pages 170-175

COLOGNES AND
FRAGRANCES
Pages 176-183

HANDS AND FEET
Pages 184-189

FACE AND SKIN
Pages 190-195

HERBS FOR THE HAIR
Pages 196-201

Bath Oils, Scrubs and Gels

hile bathing has always been a functional routine with its primary purpose to cleanse the body, it nevertheless has connotations of pleasure and relaxation. Once we discovered that bathing could be a pleasurable experience, coinciding, no doubt, with the means of getting large enough quantities of hot water easily, we found ways of making it even more enjoyable and beneficial to the body and mind. Scent, in particular, has the ability to soothe and relax us. From earliest times all kinds of ingredients have been added to bathwater to smooth and cleanse the skin, replenish lost moisture or just to soften and perfume the water. Herbs and flowers have traditionally been part of this ritual, from the days of the rose-scented baths enjoyed by the Romans to today's invigorating scrubs and gels based on herbs and natural scents.

Making your own ingredients for pleasing bathtimes is not difficult. It can be as simple as diluting some deliciously-scented essential oils into a hot bath or making special scrubs or little sachets to run under the tap. Many commercial bath additives are very harsh, as they are based on detergents which strip the skin of oils while providing the foam that people seem to like. Few of them actually moisturise. Oats and oatmeal are useful for softening and gently cleansing the skin. A small muslin bag of raw oats agitated through the warm bathwater makes a lovely silky bath to soak in. Add herbs, rose petals, and scents of other kinds and you have a truly delicious mixture.

RIGHT: Making your own bath additives is as simple as it is pleasurable. What's more, these natural preparations will help to soothe your skin, relax frayed nerves and invigorate your body.

Lemon thyme

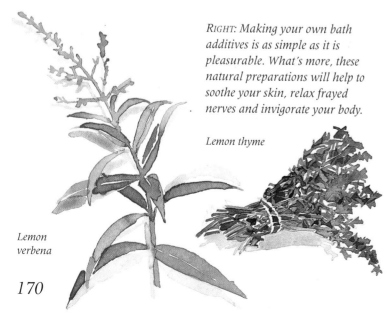

Lemon verbena

The traditional bath-time herbs have been rosemary, lavender and rose. You can experiment with different ingredients to achieve the scents and skin-treating properties you are aiming for. In many recipes you can use dried herbs very successfully and in smaller quantities than you would need for fresh herbs, but if you have access to fresh herbs then make good use of them, remembering to boost the quantities by at least twice as much. Most of the ingredients for these recipes are available from chemists if you ask for them or they can always order them, but you can also find them in specialised shops such as herbalists and some health food shops. Many of them are surprisingly inexpensive, compared with commercially-made bath additives.

Herb Bubble Bath Gel

Pure or castile soap for making this gel can be bought from good pharmacies. It contains no scent or other additives.

250ml/8fl oz water
1 tbsp sweet woodruff
1 tbsp mint
1 tbsp comfrey
1 tbsp angelica
5 tbsps pure soap
2 tbsps glycerine
2 tsps witch hazel
5 drops oil of lemon verbena
1 tbsp powdered gelatine

Makes about 350ml/12fl oz.

Angelica   Woodruff

LEFT: *This recipe makes a lovely, softening mixture which produces a nice foam if you pour it into the bath before running the water.*

1 Measure out the ingredients and boil the water.

Aromatic Bath Oil

*B*ath oils work by settling a film of oil over the surface of the bath. They do not disperse in the water unless they are in an emulsion. They leave the skin feeling very soft and can be perfumed with essential oils. Pat your skin dry after the bath; don't rub it. This mixture can be adapted, of course, by using different essential oils.

125ml/4fl oz tincture of benzoin
50ml/2fl oz avocado oil
10 drops oil of sandalwood
10 drops oil of cinnamon
10 drops oil of orange
10 drops oil of basil
10 drops oil of rosemary

Combine all the ingredients and shake thoroughly to mix them. Use 1 tbsp per bath. You can use almond or apricot oil in place of avocado.

2 Make an infusion of the herbs and the boiling water. Grate the soap.

3 Strain the infusion and discard the herbs. Add the soap, stirring well. Combine the glycerine and witch hazel and add the oil. Add this to the herb mixture.

4 When it is all thoroughly mixed, add the gelatine and stir until it is perfectly dissolved. When cool, pot the mixture into small jars.

Herbal Bath Sachets

These little sachets can be made in quantity and used one to a bath. Here they are made in a pretty fabric, but for everyday the herb mixture can simply be spooned into a square of ordinary butter-muslin and tied with string. The muslin can even be re-used once the herbs have lost their properties. To use the sachets, either throw one into the bath and leave it or hold it under the tap as the bath is run. You may find that it can be used for a second bath. This mixture is refreshing and invigorating; change the varieties of herbs, if you want a different effect. Volume measurements (250ml/8fl oz) are again used here, to ensure the correct proportions.

4 cups dried lemon verbena
2 cups dried thyme
1 cup dried peppermint
Fabric such as organdie or muslin which
allows the water to penetrate easily

1 Mix the herbs together thoroughly in a bowl. Cut out pieces of fabric to make the sachets. In this case cut an oblong which will fold into a square, leaving a little extra to make a turning at the top.

2 With the right sides of the fabric together, sew along the sides. Turn the right way out and turn down the top edge to neaten. Sew this in place. Fill with the herb mixture and tie the bag together with ribbon or cord.

Bath Scrub

*T*his mixture is designed to be rubbed briskly on to damp skin before bathing, then rinsed off. The oatmeal smoothes and softens the skin beautifully, and the thyme is marvellously refreshing and astringent. The orange and rose provide the delicious scent. To make this, you need a small coffee mill or spice grinder, so that you can obtain a fine powder from each of the various ingredients.

3 cups coarse oatmeal
1 cup dried, scented, red rose petals
1 cup dried thyme
Dried orange peel from 2 oranges

1 Measure out and prepare the ingredients. Choose a suitable, airtight container for the scrub.

2 Work in small batches grinding a mixture of the different ingredients each time.

3 Finally mix all the batches you have ground together really well before putting them into the container for storage. Store in a cool, dark place to retain its scent.

Thyme

Colognes and Fragrances

ntil quite recently no-one had thought much about the possibilities of making and creating perfumes and fragrances at home. Now that it is so much easier to buy natural essential oils there is really no difficulty in making your own fragrances. They may not have the subtlety of some of the famous name-brands from Parisian perfumeries who have access to fabulous ingredients from around the world, but they can be fresh and delightful and will cost a fraction of the price of commercial perfumes.

While perfumes might not have been frequently home-made, refreshing colognes and scented waters have a long history, from the simple rosewater splashed over a weary visitor upon arrival at a house in medieval times, to the quaint lavender-scented toilet waters and colognes favoured in Victorian times. Perfumes were often considered too sophisticated, even wicked, for many people with strict religious codes, but colognes were simple and wholesome and were therefore permitted for refreshing hot brows on summer days, dabbing inside wrists and sprinkling on handkerchiefs.

Always use totally pure essential oils, and be sure that they have not been diluted or tampered with in any way. Buy from a reputable herbalist who guarantees the authenticity of the product. A good way of checking is to see whether the oils cost different prices. Some fragrances are more costly than others to collect and produce. If they are all being sold at the same price, the expensive oils are unlikely to be pure.

Rosemary

RIGHT: Fragrances and perfumes are easy and inexpensive to create at home. They make excellent gifts for friends and family, presented in attractive bottles, trimmed with ribbon or small sprays of mixed dried herbs.

A few people have an allergic or negative reaction to certain oils applied directly to the skin. In most fragrances and colognes, the oils are very diluted but always be careful and note any strange reaction to a mixture. A few such, as bergamot (oswego or bee-balm), can have a serious photosensitive effect on the skin, even when diluted. Test it out on yourself first, and do not give it to anyone unless you are sure they will not get a reaction from it. Oil of bergamot (oswego or bee-balm) is not to be confused with oil of the bergamot orange, which is used extensively in perfumery. The scents are very similar, hence the name, but the orange oil is perfectly harmless.

Once you have tried mixing and making your own fragrances, you may find that you wish to experiment further, creating your own personal perfumes. This can be a fascinating subject and also a perfect means to making very special gifts for friends and relations. Look out for second-hand bottles in which to store your creations or save your old bottles that once contained perfumes. It is possible to buy some beautiful new bottles and containers for storing fragrances, but remember that they must have a completely airtight stopper if the contents are not to evaporate. Keep the fragrances in a cool and preferably a dark place if you wish to store them for any length of time. It is not possible to buy medicinal alcohol these days as a base for perfumes and colognes so the nearest substitute is vodka, which has no smell of its own. It is sometimes possible to find pure alcohol when abroad, which would work as well. Some Eastern European countries sell pure alcohol in their chemist shops. Most recipes are easy to make, but time is needed for the ingredients to blend and mature. Check the time required before making a recipe.

Bergamot

RIGHT: You can be quite generous in applying this citrusy splash – it is lovely as an astringent on a hot summer's day. Ideally, you would need to make this fragrance a few months in advance if you plan to make a gift of it, to allow the scent to mature fully.

Orange and Lemon Verbena Splash

*T*his is a fresh and zesty splash-on fragrance to use after a bath or shower. Orangeflower water is available from specialist food shops, herbalists and good pharmacists.

1 unwaxed orange
1 unwaxed lemon
1 cup dried lemon verbena
600ml/1 pint vodka
140 ml/5fl oz orangeflower water
10 drops oil of orange
10 drops oil of lemon verbena
5 drops oil of bergamot
5 drops oil of rose geranium

Makes about 750ml/24fl oz cologne.

Lemon verbena

1 Gather together and measure out the ingredients you need and select a suitable, airtight bottle for storing the fragrance. Rinse and dry the fruit.

2 Peel the orange and lemon and put the peel with the lemon verbena into the alcohol. Stir well, cover with clingfilm, or put into a screw-top jar and leave for about a week, shaking occasionally.

3 Strain the mixture and discard the herbs and peels.

4 Add the orangeflower water and the essential oils. Stir very thoroughly. Bottle and store for as long as possible, but do not use for at least 2 months.

Rose and Vanilla Perfume

*T*his is a rich, sweet perfume, very feminine and delicious. Oil of roses is an expensive essential oil, so you can substitute rose geranium oil if you prefer. Petitgrain oil is used in perfumery and is available from herbalists and good health shops. When using vanilla for cosmetics, always use the pure oil or extract, never the alcohol-based extract used in cooking.

70ml/3fl oz vodka
15ml/1 tbsp rosewater
1 cup scented dried rose petals
2 vanilla pods
10 drops oil of roses
10 drops oil of vanilla
10 drops petitgrain oil
5 drops oil of ylang-ylang

Rose

1 Measure out the vodka and the scented dried rose petals, or pull the petals off the roses if they are whole flower heads.

2 Crush the vanilla pods and steep them with the rose petals in the vodka. Cover and leave for a week.

3 Strain the vodka and add the rosewater. Stir very well.

4 Add the drops of essential oils, stirring constantly. Bottle and leave to mature for about four weeks. Strain again through filter paper and bottle before using.

Lime Skin Freshener for Men

*T*his is a citrus-based, scented, splash-on cologne to be used on the face or body. The limes must be as fresh as possible, or the oils in the skins will have evaporated. You will need:

2 fresh limes
250ml/8fl oz vodka
15 drops oil of lime
10 drops petitgrain oil
5 drops oil of lavender
5 drops oil of bergamot
5 drops oil of bayleaf
1 tsp benzoin tincture
250ml/8fl oz rosewater

RIGHT: Benzoin tincture is added to this cologne to act as both a preservative and an astringent. It is also a mild antiseptic.

Bay

1 Gather together all the ingredients and put to one side, except for the vodka and the limes. Measure out the vodka into a container.

2 Peel the limes and put the peel into the vodka. Cover and leave to steep for a week.

3 Put the drops of essential oil and the benzoin into the rosewater, and stir very well. Strain the vodka and discard the lime peel. Mix the rosewater with the vodka. Stir very well and bottle. Leave for four weeks. Strain again through a paper filter, then bottle finally before use.

Lavender

Rosemary

Eau de Cologne

This is lovely to use generously whenever you need to freshen up. There are several versions of the traditional recipe and ideally they need neroli oil which is expensive but you don't need very much of it.

12 drops oil of bergamot
12 drops oil of lemon
20 drops oil of orange
3 drops neroli oil
3 drops oil of rosemary
2 drops oil of basil
100ml/4fl oz vodka
30ml/2 tbsps spring water

Add the oils to the vodka and stir well. Cover and leave to stand for 48 hours. Add the spring water and stir again. Leave another 48 hours or up to four weeks if you can wait. Stir and strain through filter paper. Dilute with more water if it seems too strong. Bottle and use.

Hands and Feet

Hands and feet are the hard-working parts of our bodies which seem to be the most neglected. While we lavish care and attention on our faces and bodies, our feet, in particular, are often more-or-less ignored. Hands suffer doubly from the normal everyday exposure to the cold, the sun's harmful rays and alongside this, all the harsh substances such as detergents which we use almost without stopping to think of the damage they do. Herbs are extremely helpful in alleviating this damage and in providing some of the luxurious cosmetics that improve the condition of hard-working hands and feet.

For centuries, people have soothed tired and aching feet in a hot foot bath scented with herbs and spiced with other ingredients. Peppermint and eucalyptus both have a marvellous invigorating effect on the feet, pepping up the circulation and leaving a warm tingling glow. It is very easy to make a quick foot bath at the end of a long day by adding a few drops of essential oil to warm water. Some herbs that are beneficial to the feet are marigold to help soften hard or calloused skin, and fennel, lavender and chamomile to help reduce the swelling in swollen feet. Geranium essential oil is great for improving the elasticity of skin on the feet, and it boosts the circulation which is important in keeping chilblains at bay in the winter.

Hands are more likely to need serious nourishment, rather than an invigorating treatment. Nails and cuticles are particular problem areas. Many old-fashioned hand-creams were designed to bleach and keep the hands soft and white.

RIGHT: Herbs have much to offer in being able to nourish hard-working hands and feet, and to heal and protect them, when applied in home-made creams, gels and baths.

Rose

We are unlikely to worry about freckles much nowadays, but it is sensible to screen the skin on hands from too much sun, as they show signs of ageing earlier than any other part of the body. Elderflower and chamomile are traditional herbs for the hands and so are rose, lavender, marigold and geranium. Combined with rich oils and creams, these can do much to improve the texture of the skin on the hands. If you spend a lot of time doing heavy, messy work, such as gardening, then you will need all the help you can get. Try to remember to wear a barrier cream or salve on the hands before starting work, and use gloves whenever possible. At the end of the day, treat hands to a rich cream, and go to bed wearing cotton gloves.

Almond and Rose Hand Cream

*T*his is quite a thick cream, designed to be slowly massaged into the hands at the end of a hard day. For other times use a much smaller quantity and rub it in really well until it has been absorbed. Becuase this hand cream contains almond oil, it will also be beneficial to the nails, if regularly applied.

3 tbsps almond oil
3 tbsps coconut oil
2 tbsps white beeswax granules
4 tbsps glycerine
5 drops oil of roses or rose geranium
10 drops evening primrose oil

1 *Measure out the ingredients and fill the lower part of a double-boiler or a saucepan with water. Place over low heat.*

2 *Melt the almond oil, coconut oil and beeswax in a bowl over the saucepan of simmering water.*

Rosemary

3 *Add the glycerine, drop by drop, stirring until you have a creamy mass.*

4 *Add the essential oils, beat well and pour into clean jars.*

Sage

LEFT: *If you are hard on your hands, it is worth making up several jars of this rich hand cream, so that you can keep a ready supply wherever you wash your hands.*

Rosemary, Lavender and Sage Foot Cream

*T*his is perfect for rough, dry skin on feet. Rub it in well after a softening foot bath. Use beeswax granules if you can find them, as they dissolve much faster than large solid blocks of beeswax which have to be grated to melt quickly.

2 tbsps white beeswax granules
2 tbsps cocoa butter
6 tbsps apricot kernel oil
10 drops oil of rosemary
10 drops oil of lavender
10 drops oil of sage
15 drops evening primrose oil

Melt the beeswax and cocoa butter in the top half of a double-boiler over boiling water, stirring gently until the wax has dissolved completely. Warm the apricot oil in another small pan and add it slowly to the first mixture, beating constantly. Remove from the heat and add the essential oils and evening primrose oil. Pour into small jars or tins and store in a cool dark place to keep it fresh.

Elderflower and Chamomile Hand Gel

*T*his gentle, soothing yellow gel is excellent for softening hands without making them feel greasy.

3 tbsps arrowroot
100ml/4fl oz water
2 tbsps dried chamomile
2 tbsps dried elderflowers
3 tbsps glycerine

Chamomile

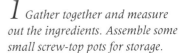

1 Gather together and measure out the ingredients. Assemble some small screw-top pots for storage.

3 Warm the glycerine in a double-boiler and add the arrowroot. Stir very well.

LEFT: *Chamomile has many healing and cosmetic uses. This hand gel exploits the herb's ability to soften the skin. Elderflower is effective as a tonic for all skins.*

Walnut, Bay and Balm Foot Bath

Make a strong infusion of fresh herbs by steeping about 10 cups of herbs in 1 litre/1¾ pints of boiling water until cool. Include as many of the following as possible: walnut leaves, bay, rosemary, lavender, sage and lemon balm. Strain the liquid and whisk in a tablespoon of grated castile soap to 1 litre/1¾ pints of infusion. Add a few drops of rosemary and bay essential oils and soak the feet for at least 10 minutes. Pat them dry and rub in some nourishing foot cream or plain almond oil, while the feet are still warm. Put on a pair of clean cotton socks and sit with your feet up for a while. To gain the maximum benefit from the herbal foot bath, retire to your bed and lie with your feet slightly raised on a pillow.

2 *Heat the water and add the herbs. Leave to steep until thoroughly cooled.*

4 *Strain the infusion. Gradually add to the glycerine and arrowroot mixture and stir until it is clear and starting to gel. Put into the pots.*

Walnut

Face and Skin

*H*erbs can do wonders for the skin of the face or body. Our skin needs every bit of help it can get because though many of us eat better food than previous generations our skin is subjected to increasingly dangerous sunlight, air pollution from all around us and the strains of a generally too stressful lifestyle. Skin and hair are the first indicators of being out of condition and though we all know we should exercise more, eat healthier foods and drink less alcohol, get more fresh air and so on, few of us do anything about it! Herbs play a part in healing damaged skin and a second more subtle role in lifting the spirits and soothing the mind, which greatly affects the way we ultimately look. Many people would rather use products made from plain, wholesome ingredients and even many of the cosmetic and beauty houses are trying to provide these, even in their most high-tech ranges of products.

Many of the simplest and most old-fashioned remedies are the best, for example rosewater and witch hazel has been used for decades as a mild toner and skin freshener. It could not be easier to make and is so much cheaper than a commercial alternative. Ingredients for all these recipes are generally available from dispensing chemists. Very often they can order them for you and get ingredients which are not on the shelves. Otherwise, find a herbalist or company which will send ingredients by mail. As there is a renewed interest in making cosmetics at home many ingredients are easier to find than they once were.

RIGHT: Herbs can be used effectively in a whole range of skin preparations, including lotions and creams, astringents and masks, scrubs, cleansers, night and day creams, steam treatments and compresses.

Making creams and lotions is fun and generally quite easy, though you will improve with practise. Understanding the process of obtaining an emulsion is important. A lotion or cream is an emulsion of various oils in a non-oily base. Often a liquid such as rosewater is added to the melted oils, drop by drop, rather like making mayonnaise. As the water-based liquid meets and mixes with the warm oils, they emulsify and turn opaque and creamy. This is the process which is used for many recipes. It is really fascinating to see it happening the first time. Occasionally things go wrong, usually because temperatures or proportions are not right, but this is quite rare.

Rose and lavender are two herbs that are frequently used for skin preparations, as are marigold, elderflower and chamomile. Others, from a very long list, include fennel, carrot and geranium.

Rosewater and Witch Hazel Toner

*H*arsh astringents and toners can do more harm than good but if you use a cream cleanser, the skin cries out for a cooling tonic to finish off. This one is exactly right. It has been used for centuries and one can see why. Find a source of good-quality rosewater. Chemist shops often sell it quite cheaply.

1 tbsp vodka
2 tbsps glycerine
200ml/8fl oz rosewater
100ml/4fl oz witch hazel

Mix the vodka with the glycerine and stir very well. Pour into the rosewater and add the witch hazel, bottle and shake until well blended. Shake the bottle each time before using. Sprinkle on cotton-wool pads and dab gently onto the face.

Simple Mint Cleanser

Eau-de-cologne mint

This is cooling, soothing and deliciously scented. You can make it in a liquidiser if you prefer. Made this way, even after straining, some tiny shreds of mint may remain in the mixture, so rinse the face well after use. Sprinkle it on a cotton-wool pad and rub it over your skin instead of soap. It is particularly good to use if you have a delicate skin.

300ml/10fl oz fresh milk
4 tbsps fresh mint (apple, eau-de-cologne or peppermint)

1 Measure out the milk and pour into a clean bowl. Wash the mint and dry.

2 Chop the mint finely and add it to the milk. Leave to infuse in the refrigerator for about 12 hours.

3 Strain the liquid and bottle it. Store it in the refrigerator.

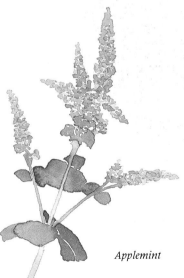

Applemint

Apricot and Orange Moisturiser

This is a fairly rich cream for the skin of the face or body. If you want to tint it, use a tiny amount of a natural food colouring to make it a pale apricot colour. You will need:

2 tsps white beeswax granules
4 tbsps apricot kernel oil
2 tbsps coconut oil
2 tbsps glycerine
2 tbsps orangeflower water
3 drops oil of orange

1 Gather all the ingredients together and measure out the beeswax granules.

2 Melt the beeswax and apricot kernel and coconut oils in the top half of a double-boiler, over hot water, stirring until they are completely dissolved.

Left: Orangeflower water is good for dry skin and stimulates cell replacement.

3 Add the glycerine to the beeswax and oils, and stir thoroughly. Warm the orangeflower water separately.

4 Remove the double-boiler from the heat and add the orangeflower water drop by drop, beating all the time until it is a smooth cream. Add the oil of orange and stir well. Add colouring if you wish. Pot into small jars.

ABOVE: Steam your face for about 10 mintues over the rose or herb infusion of your choice. Then refresh the skin with a clean, damp facecloth. Your skin will feel cleansed and revitalised.

Fennel

Rose Steam Treatment

One of the simplest of all beauty treatments is a herbal steam bath, to open the pores and deep cleanse the skin. It is like a sauna for the face, with the added bonus of scented beneficial herbs to do the soothing and healing. If your skin is very blemished or delicate, do not attempt a steam treatment. Ordinary and oily skins will benefit from regular steam baths. Simply mix a handful or two of fresh or dried herbs of your choice in a bowl of very hot water. Let them infuse a few seconds then put your face over them and cover your head with a towel to keep the heat in. Roses make the most delicious treatment, especially if you can use fresh, highly-scented roses from the garden in summer. Alternatively, try basil, chamomile or marigold, or create a mixture such as a combination of fennel and lavender.

Herbs for the Hair

While nothing does as much as a good cut for a beautiful head of hair, how you wash it and the products you put on it have a very important effect too. In the days before mass-produced shampoos and conditioners, people had to concoct these things from ingredients found easily in the home and, as in other branches of housekeeping, sensible women turned to herbs. From leaves, stems and flowers found wild or cultivated in the garden they made lotions and washes which were functional but added gloss or natural-looking colour to the hair. Certain herbs have always been connected with healthy hair and scalp, such as willow, horsetail, rosemary, yarrow, nettle and chamomile.

These days, we wash our hair more frequently than our ancestors did, and need to take special care of its condition. To ensure you have the glossiest hair, wash it in a gentle shampoo and rinse and rinse until no trace is left. Restoring a slightly acid balance to the hair after using alkaline products is another key factor in improving its look. Of course, it goes without saying that a healthy lifestyle and good diet will do more for the hair from the inside than anything applied from the outside.

At one time, it was thought that certain herbs could cure baldness and increase the growth of hair. It is highly unlikely that anything was really able to do this but certain herbs definitely stimulate the blood circulation to the skin of the scalp and perhaps have led to the belief that the hair was growing more luxuriantly. Most men these days use the same kinds of hair products as women do but a century or two ago, there were all manner of special brilliantines, pomades, tonics and rubs for the man who cared about his appearance.

Soapwort

RIGHT: Treat your hair and scalp to the attention they deserve by using a home-made herbal shampoo or rinse as a natural and gentle substitute for a commercially-produced product.

Soapwort (*Saponaria officinalis*) is an interesting herb which gained its name from the fact that it works as a gentle shampoo or cleanser for hair and textiles. The roots and leaves of the soapwort are used to produce a liquid which lathers and removes grease and dirt. It has been used since Roman times and probably even earlier. It is possible to buy the plant dried to use in making natural shampoos.

Elderflower Rinse

Rinsing the hair and removing every trace of shampoo is an important part of achieving shiny and truly clean hair. This basic recipe for a rinse could be made with chamomile instead if you prefer. If used frequently, chamomile will have a gentle and slight, but progressive, bleaching effect on mousey or blonde hair. Keep a bottle of this liquid in the bathroom and pour some over the hair as the very last rinse.

2 litres/3½ pints water
2 handfuls dried elderflowers or
4 handfuls of fresh flowers
1 lemon

2 Boil the water and pour it over the elderflowers in the bowl. Stir it thoroughly and leave to infuse until cold. Squeeze the juice of the lemon and strain it.

1 Gather your ingredients together. Place the flowers in a large bowl.

3 Strain the liquid and discard the elderflowers. Add the strained lemon juice and mix well. Pour into bottles and cork securely. Use a cupful or so as a final rinse.

Soapwort and Egg Shampoo

*T*his is mild and gentle and excellent for any hair type. Be sure to rinse out every trace.

250ml/8fl oz water
1 tbsp dried soapwort
1 egg yolk
Juice of one lemon, strained

Boil the water and pour it over the soapwort. Stir well, then leave to infuse and cool down. Whisk the egg yolk and strained lemon juice together and add to the cooled soapwort infusion. Store in the refrigerator.

Box and Bay Hair Tonic

*T*his robust tonic is designed for men. It should strengthen the hair and stimulate the scalp. It can be used as a rinse, or simply brushed through the hair between washes. Use fresh box leaves and bay if you can; it may be hard to find dried box. If you cannot get hold of box, then substitute dried yarrow or fennel to go with the bay leaves. You will need:

1 cup bay leaves
1 cup box leaves
2 litres/3½ pints water
150ml/5fl oz eau de cologne
150ml/5fl oz cider vinegar

Box

1 Gather together and measure out all the ingredients you require. Select a bottle that can be made airtight for storing the tonic.

2 *Strip off the leaves and put them into a pan. Add water and bring to the boil. Simmer for 20 minutes. Leave to cool.*

Sage and Rosemary Rinse

*T*his rinse is meant for brunettes. Used often, it adds lustre and depth to dark hair colour. Fresh herbs are pleasant to use but you can also use dried ones. Make it in the same way as the elderflower rinse but use 100ml/3½fl oz cider vinegar in place of the lemon juice and a handful of each of the herbs, or two handfuls each if they are fresh. Rosemary is supposed to help prevent dandruff and other scalp problems. It is slightly antiseptic.

3 *Strain the liquid from the leaves which you should discard. Add the eau de cologne to the vinegar and then pour this mixture into the herb mixture. Bottle. Shake well each time before using.*

Herbal Information

HARVESTING AND
PRESERVING HERBS
Pages 204-207

A REFERENCE GUIDE
TO HERBS
Pages 208-215

HERB SOURCES
Pages 216-217

INDEX
Pages 218-219

CREDITS
Pages 220

Harvesting and Preserving Herbs

resh herb leaves and flowers add flavour and colour to salads and a variety of other dishes as well as beauty and fragrance to the home in the form of decorations and arrangements. Although it is usually far better to use fresh rather than dried herbs in cooking to reap their full benefits, this is normally only possible during summer. In the past, before the days of advanced farming techniques and imported fruit and vegetables, drying herbs was one of the few ways to preserve the flavours of summer for the coming winter months, and this is still the next best option to using fresh herbs. Dried herb flowers and foliage may not be comparable to the fresh items in season, but they are pretty and decorative in their own, different way, and can be used to create long-lasting displays and decorations. When infused, some dried herbs release their preserved aromatic flavours to make delicious and therapeutic teas and tisanes, while other highly-scented dried herbs can be used in pot pourris or to fill sachets for perfuming clothes in storage. Dried herbs can also be very successfully used in a variety of bath and beauty preparations, and in smaller quantities than would be needed if you were using fresh herbs.

Herbs that dry well and retain their flavour, fragrance and potency are those that grow as fairly shrubby plants, such as rosemary, thyme, bay, sage and marjoram. Other herbs can be dried, but lose the fullness of their flavour and aroma in the process, so must be used in extra quantities in recipes when dried. These include parsley, mint, tarragon, chervil, fennel and dill. Herbs that are herbaceous, such as chives, borage, basil and balm are rather less successful when dried, so use them fresh whenever possible.

If you plan to use the herb's leaves, these should be harvested just as the plants come into flower and before the seeds form to preserve them at their best. Gather the herbs in the morning as soon as the dew has evaporated and before the warmth of the sun has begun to draw out the oils that give them their flavour and aroma and they begin to wilt in the heat of the day. Discard any old or discoloured leaves or any that have been damaged by insects. This is especially important if you will be using the leaves decoratively as the appearance will be spoiled.

Herb flowers for display are best harvested at midday in dry weather. Cut the stems just before the flowers are about to open fully. Pick them carefully to avoid damaging the petals of the flowers.

Herbs need to be dried as quickly as possible in order to preserve their flavour and colour. However, drying them in direct sunlight will damage them. They can be dried in several different ways. Individual leaves and flowers can be placed on

Lovage

204

RIGHT: Sprigs of dried bay are excellent for use in displays but for cooking it is better to use the fresh leaves.

BELOW: Many herbs keep their flavour and fragrance well when dried. In a few cases, their potency is enhanced through drying.

Fennel

trays covered with absorbent kitchen paper or on wire cooling racks, and left in a warm, dry and dark place, such as an airing cupboard. Alternatively, heat the oven on its lowest setting and place the herbs inside to dry. Check regularly to make sure they do not burn.

A pretty and traditional way to dry whole stems of herbs, especially flowering and decorative herbs for display, is to air-dry them. Strip the lower leaves from the stems and group them into bunches. Tie the stems together with a long length of string and hang the bunches upside down in a warm, dry, dark place to dry. Do not leave the bunches there indefinitely, though, as the herbs can become dusty and lose their flavour and fragrance after some time.

One of the quickest ways to dry herb leaves is to use the microwave; results with flowers are variable. Strip the leaves from the stems and place them in a single layer on a sheet of absorbent kitchen paper. Cook on HIGH for 30 seconds, then turn the leaves over and cook for a further 30 seconds to 1 minute, checking at 5-second intervals to be sure that the leaves don't burn. A note of caution – older-model microwaves can be damaged by this process. Consult your machine's instructions or manufacturer before attempting to use it to dry herbs.

To store the dried herb leaves, strip them from their stalks if necessary and put them into screw-top jars or cloth bags. Label the jars carefully – herbs tend to look similar when dried and it is easy to forget which is which. Keep them in a dark place. To help preserve their flavour, do not crumble the leaves of culinary herbs until just before you want to use them.

The colour and shape of individual flowers can be best preserved by using silica gel crystals, but only for decorative purposes, not culinary. Roses are particularly suitable for this treatment. Place a 2.5 cm (1 inch) layer of dry silica gel crystals in an airtight container, then carefully position the flower heads. Spoon over further crystals until the flowers are completely covered. Put the lid on the container and leave in a warm, dry place for two to three days. Remove the flowers carefully as they will be brittle.

Dried herb seeds, such as coriander, dill and aniseed often have a quite distinctive, spicy favour, and are an essential ingredient in certain dishes, pickles and drinks. Caraway and poppy seeds are used to give flavour and to decorate cakes and breads. To dry the seeds, cut the seed-heads from the plant just as they begin to turn brown. Place the seed-heads in large paper bags and leave to dry in a warm room. As the seeds dry, they will fall out of the seed-head to the bottom of the paper bag. Store the seeds in glass jars out of direct light.

RIGHT: Herbs tied into bunches with pretty ribbon and hung up in the kitchen to air-dry make a really pleasing, country display.

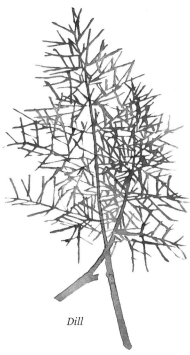

Dill

LEFT: Delicate herb leaves, such as dill, parsley, fennel, mint, tarragon and chervil, are best preserved by freezing, to keep their colour and flavour.

Fresh herbs can be frozen, although the majority of herbs become limp when thawed. The most suitable herbs are those such as parsley, dill and fennel, which tend to lose some of their flavour when dried. Wash the herbs and dry them thoroughly. Tie them into small bunches and place them in polythene bags. Seal the bags to make them airtight and place them in the freezer. When required, the frozen bunches of herbs can be added directly to casseroles and soups. Herbs such as parsley can be crumbled while still frozen.

An attractive way to freeze small portions of herbs is to freeze them in ice cubes. This is particularly useful for adding to summer drinks, punches and fruit cups. Suitable herbs include mint and salad burnet leaves and colourful borage flowers, all of which will give subtle flavour. Simply place the herbs in an ice cube tray and fill with water, then place in the freezer as usual. Use mineral water for a clear effect, as tap water tends to go cloudy when frozen.

Another way to preserve the flavours of fresh herbs is to use them to make herb vinegars that can be added to salad dressings and sauces. Suitable herbs include tarragon, basil and garlic (see page 78). Herb flowers such as marigold, elderflower and chives can also be preserved by steeping them in vinegar in this way, giving a more delicate flavour to the liquid. These vinegars look attractive on display in the kitchen and make interesting gifts too.

Herbs can be stored in salt, and this method is useful for herbs that do not dry well, such as basil. Starting with a layer of salt at the bottom of an airtight jar, add alternate layers of salt and herb leaves, finishing with a final layer of salt. When you use the leaves, simply shake or rinse them.

Herbs can also be preserved in butter. Simply chop the herbs and beat them into butter with a little seasoning and lemon juice. Parsley, chervil, chives and tarragon are suitable, or a mixture of herbs. The butter can be placed in ice cube trays in the freezer, then used as a garnish for snacks and vegetables, releasing the full flavour of the herbs as it melts.

The flowers, leaves and stems of some herbs can be decorative and tasty additions to cakes and desserts or eaten on their own as sweetmeats. Dainty violet flowers retain both their colour and taste well when crystallised. Simply coat the flowers lightly with beaten egg white, then dip them into caster sugar. Dry them gently in a slow oven or leave them in a warm airing cupboard between layers of greaseproof paper. When they are completely dry store them in an airtight tin. Rose petals and borage flowers can also be preserved by this method, as can mint and scented geranium leaves.

Angelica stalks can be candied for use in decorating cakes and trifles. These delicious sweetmeats take on a characteristic bright green colour when boiled in syrup with green leaves. You will find a recipe on page 79. Store the candied angelica in an airtight tin.

A Reference Guide to Herbs

Allium sativum
GARLIC

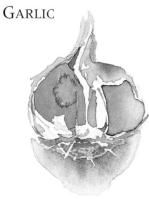

Garlic has thin, bright green leaves which grow from the sheath of a slender cylindrical stem. It grows to a height of about 30 cm (12 in) and its globe-shaped flower head contains small white florets. Garlic is a hardy perennial and grows from a bulb which is divided up into cloves. The distinctive flavour of the bulb is used widely in cooking. Garlic prefers a well-drained rich, moist soil in a sunny position

Allium schoenoprasum
CHIVES

Chives grow in clumps up to 15–25 cm (6–10 in) high with

bright green, thin cylindrical stems topped with large pink or mauve pompom flowers in midsummer. Often used for garnishing food, their delicate oniony flavour is used in salads and soft cheeses and the flowers add colour to herb vinegars. Chives prefer a rich, damp soil and should be grown in a sunny position, but make sure they do not dry out.

Aloysia triphylla
LEMON VERBENA, HERB LOUISA

Lemon verbena is a fragrant, perennial shrub which produces masses of pale purple or white flowers. Its slender green leaves smell strongly of lemon and they can be used fresh in fruit salads, punches and fruit cups, or dried and added to pot pourris and bath preparations. Lemon verbena can grow to a height of 1.5 cm (5 ft) if planted in a warm, sheltered spot.

Anethum graveolens
DILL

Dill is a fragrant hardy annual with fine, feathery green leaves and small, deep yellow flowers

growing in flat heads. The plant will grow to a height of 60–90 cm (2–3 ft). The leaves are often used in savoury sauces to accompany fish, or chopped and added to salads. The seeds can be used in stews, soups, vinegars and pickles. Dill prefers a sunny position and fine, well-drained soil.

Angelica archangelica
ANGELICA

Angelica is a large biennial herb with glossy green leaves and self-seeding white flowers. It is a hardy plant which can grow to a height of 1–2 m (3-6 ft). Angelica is best known for its candied form, with the bright green stems used to decorate cakes, but its sweet leaves can be used to flavour preserves or fruit dishes. Angelica thrives in wetter climates, growing well in rich soil and partially shaded areas.

Anthriscus cerefolium
CHERVIL

Chervil is a fern-like plant and grows to a height of about 45 cm (18 in). It has pale green leaves and small white flowers, and both flat and curly-leaved varieties are available. Combined with parsley, tarragon and thyme, chervil is one of the classic *fine herbes* used in French cooking. It has a subtle aniseed flavour and can be used in salads and soups. Chervil prefers a well-drained, partially shady site.

Artemisia abrotanum
SOUTHERNWOOD, FIELD SOUTHERNWOOD, ARTEMISIA

Southernwood is a woody perennial with grey-green

feathery leaves which, when crushed, have a lemon scent. The plant sometimes produces small yellow flowers and will grow to a height of 1 m (3 ft) if cut back. When dried, the leaves can be added to linen sachets as they will repel moths and other insects. Southernwood thrives in light, well-drained soil in a sunny position.

Artemisia dracunculus
TARRAGON, FRENCH TARRAGON

Tarragon is a bushy, perennial herb with slender, aromatic green leaves. The plant produces small white flowers in late summer and can grow to a height of 1 m (3 ft). Fresh tarragon can be added to salads and vegetable dishes and used to flavour mayonnaise, jellies, vinegars and liqueurs. Tarragon prefers good, well-drained soil and a sunny position. It also grows well in pots and containers.

Borage officinalis
BORAGE

One of the prettiest herbs to grow, borage has abundant sky blue or pink star-shaped flowers with distinctive black centres. The flowers and leaves may be used to flavour liqueurs, to decorate summer drinks and to add colour to fresh herb posies. Borage is an annual herb and grows quickly from seed to become a large, sprawling plant, reaching a height of 45–75 cm (18–30 in). It will thrive in a poor chalky or sandy soil with plenty of sun.

Buxus sempervirens
BOX

Box is a hardy evergreen tree with dense, small, dark green, glossy leaves. It is slow growing but can reach a height of 4.5–6 m (15–20 ft), though it is often used for low hedging and for decorative topiary. The evergreen leaves and branches are attractive in floral and herbal decorations and the leaves can also be used to make a hair tonic. Box prefers a well-drained soil.

Calendula officinalis
MARIGOLD

Marigold is a popular hardy annual grown from seed and its brightly coloured orange or yellow flowers add cheer to any garden. The fresh flowers can be scattered over salads and dried flowers added to pot pourri to give vibrant colour.

Marigold helps to soften calloused skin and is used in beauty preparations. It will thrive in a sunny position and prefers a moist, rich soil. Dead head the plants frequently to encourage new flowers.

Carum carvi
CARAWAY

Caraway is a biennial plant with a slender, pale green, furrowed stem and feathery leaves. Its delicate flower heads bear tiny white florets and the plant grows to a height of 40–60 cm (1.5–2 ft). The aromatic seeds are used to flavour cakes and breads and may also be added to a variety of meat dishes. Caraway prefers a well-drained, light soil and a sunny position.

Thuja occidentalis
CEDARWOOD, YELLOW CEDAR

This conifer is the tallest of this species of cedar tree and can grow to a height of 9.5 m (30 ft). Its pungent aroma is similar to balsam and has the property of acting as an insect repellent, so the wood has traditionally been used to make wardrobes and chests. Cedarwood shavings can be used to make scented sachets and pot pourris, while the essential oil is used to impregnate wooden shapes.

Chamaemelum nobile
CHAMOMILE

Chamomile is an annual herb with small, scented yellow and white flowers. It has a great many healing and cosmetic uses. Fresh or dried leaves make a soothing tea to settle indigestion, and a simple infusion of chamomile flowers makes a good herbal rinse for fair hair. Chamomile is very easy to grow from seeds sown in early spring, preferring a dry, sunny position and light, well-drained soil.

Coriandrum sativum
CORIANDER

Coriander is an easy-to-grow hardy annual. Its lower leaves are bright green and look similar to flat-leaf parsley, while the upper leaves are feathery. The plant grows to a height of 60 cm (2 ft) and has small, pinkish-white flowers. The aromatic seeds are used to flavour foods, while the leaves have a sharp taste and can be added to salads and vegetable dishes. Coriander prefers a light, rich soil and a sunny position.

Crataegus monogyna
HAWTHORN, MAY, MAY BLOSSOM

The thorny deciduous hawthorn tree can grow to a height of 7 m (23 ft). It has mid-green, lobed leaves and bears white flowers in late spring, followed by red berries or 'haws' in early autumn. The freshly picked blossom can be used to flavour brandy and liqueurs. A fast-growing tree, hawthorn prefers a sunny, open position and is often used as decorative hedging.

Dianthus sp.
PINK, CLOVE PINK

There are several *Dianthus* species. They have long, thin leaves and jointed stems. The attractive scented flowers have serrated petals, sometimes picotee-edged, in a wide range of colours. The flowers can be used fresh in flower arrangements and posies or dried for use in pot pourris. They can also be used to flavour and decorate salads, and to flavour sugar, vinegars and wine. *Dianthus* prefers a well-drained soil and an open, sunny position.

Eucalyptus globulus
EUCALYPTUS

Eucalyptus is an evergreen tree with grey-green leaves. It is an easy-to-grow tree and can reach a height of 90 m (300 ft). The rounded leaves of the juvenile tree are used in flower arrangements and garlands and the dried leaves may be added to give colour and scent to pot pourris. Eucalyptus may be used in foot treatments as it peps up the circulation. Oil is extracted from the leaves for medicinal use.

Foeniculum vulgare
FENNEL

Fennel is a hardy perennial with aromatic, feathery leaves which can be either green or bronze in colour. From midsummer the plant produces bright yellow flowers. The leaves and seeds can be used to give a sweet aniseed flavour to food. Its health-giving properties are of use in skin and hair preparations. Fennel grows to a height of 1.5–2 m (5–6 ft) and prefers a well-drained soil and plenty of sun.

Gallium odoratum
SWEET WOODRUFF

Woodruff has delicate white flowers which bloom in early summer and narrow leaves which grow in star-shaped ruff formations. It is a low-growing plant, rarely reaching more than 20 cm (8 in) in height. Its dried leaves have the sweet smell of new-mown hay, making it an attractive addition to bath gel and herb bags. The flowers are used to flavour summer drinks. Woodruff grows well in moist, rich soil in partial shade.

Humulus lupulus
HOP

The hop is a perennial vine. It produces yellowish-green female 'cones' which contain flowers and embryonic fruits. When dried, these parts of the plant are used to flavour beer. The young shoots and immature leaves can be added to vegetable soups or cooked on their own. Hops have a slight sedative effect and the dried flowers are a traditional ingredient in herbal sleep cushions. Hops need plenty of sun and a rich soil to thrive.

Hyssopus officinalis
HYSSOP

Hyssop has aromatic, dark green leaves and woody stems, and during its long growing season produces pink, blue and white flowers. An evergreen perennial, it grows to a height of 30–60 cm (1 –2 ft). Hyssop has a strong, minty taste and smell and can be used fresh or dried in herbal insect repellents, posies and pot pourris. It prefers a sunny position and light, well-drained soil.

Jasminum sp.
JASMINE

There are many forms of Jasmine, some of which are evergreen, and most are climbing plants. The summer-flowering *Jasminum officinale* bears small white sweetly scented blossoms, while the winter-flowering *Jasminum nudiflorum* has yellow flowers.

The flowers are used to make fragrant scent sachets and pot pourris. Oil extracted from jasmine can also be used to scent candles. *Jasminum sambac* is the variety used to scent tea. Small varieties are available to be grown as pot plants or in conservatories.

Juglans regia
WALNUT

The walnut is a deciduous tree with a wide-spreading crown of large, bright green oval-shaped leaves. It produces edible nuts and can grow to a height of 8 m (30 ft). Ripe nuts can be eaten on their own or added to flavour cakes and sauces, while the green nuts can be pickled in vinegar. Their skins are used to make a rinse for dark hair and walnut leaves are used in a soothing foot bath. Walnut prefers a well-drained chalky soil.

Laurus nobilis
BAY, LAUREL, SWEET BAY

Bay is an evergreen tree with glossy green leaves and small, creamy white flowers. Although slow growing, it can grow up to 8 m (26 ft) in height. Bay leaves are one of the herbs used in the classic *bouquet garni*. A useful culinary herb, bay can also be used fresh or dried in beauty preparations and in decorative arrangements and pot pourris. Bay prefers a sheltered, sunny position and rich, well-drained soil.

Lavandula angustifolia
LAVENDER

There are many varieties of lavender ranging from dark purple to mauve, pink and white. A hardy, evergreen shrub, it grows as a compact bush up to 75 cm (30 in) in height. The clean smell of lavender is a traditional fragrance with a wide range of cosmetic and decorative uses in scented sachets, bath preparations and skin lotions. Lavender will thrive in poor but well-drained soil in a sunny position.

Melissa officinalis
LEMON BALM, MELISSA

Lemon balm is a hardy, aromatic perennial. Its pale green or variegated leaves both taste and smell of lemon. It

grows to a height of 60–100 cm (2-3 ft) and produces pale yellow or white flowers throughout the summer. Fresh lemon balm leaves make a refreshing tea and they enhance the flavour of lemonade and herb jellies. The plant prefers poor, moist soil and a sunny position.

Mentha sp.
MINT

There are many varieties of mint, all of which grow invasively and need to be contained. Mint is used for culinary and medicinal purposes. Fresh or dried leaves make a refreshing tea, and mint is traditionally used in sauces and jellies accompanying lamb. Beauty treatments based on mint cool the skin. Mint prefers to grow in moist, well-drained soil in partial shade or sun.

Mentha piperata
PEPPERMINT

Peppermint has the strongest flavour of all the mint varieties. It is widely grown commercially for many medicinal and cosmetic uses, such as toothpaste. Its leaves make a refreshing herbal tea, and dried leaves keep their flavour well. Peppermint tones up the circulation and makes a good treatment for tired or swollen feet. It is one of the most important essential oils. Peppermint thrives in a fairly warm, moist climate and prefers open textured, well-drained soils.

Mentha pulegium
PENNYROYAL, RUN-BY-THE-GROUND, LURK-IN-THE-DITCH

Pennyroyal is quite unlike other varieties of the mint family. Rather than producing a bushy plant, it grows as a low-lying, creeping half-hardy perennial, making it ideal ground cover. It has a strong flavour and smell so should only be used sparingly in cookery, but may be used in liqueurs. Pennyroyal is traditionally regarded as a flea repellent, and the fresh leaves may be rubbed into a pet's coat as a remedy. It will grow in any type of soil but prefers moist conditions.

Mentha suaveolens rotundifolia
APPLEMINT

Applemint has less invasive growing habits than other varieties of mint. Its rounded leaves have an apple scent and its milder, sweeter taste makes it ideal for use in cakes and in dishes and drinks using fruit. The dried leaves retain their scent well and fresh sprigs look attractive in aromatic herb posies. Applemint can grow to a height of 60 cm (2 ft) and thrives in rich, moist soil and partial shade.

Monarda didyma
BERGAMOT, OSWEGO, BEE BALM

Bergamot is a fragrant herb with distinctive bright red

flowers which attract bees. It can grow to a height of 45–100 cm (18–36 in). The dried leaves can be infused as a tea and oil of bergamot used to scent candles and colognes. Care should be taken, however, as skin reactions can occur in some people. Bergamot prefers a rich, moist soil and partial shade and needs to be kept well watered.

Ocimum basilicum
BASIL

Growing to a height of 30–60 cm (1–2 ft), basil has large shiny leaves and small white flowers. It is best known for its culinary uses, especially with tomatoes and as the basis for pesto sauce. This is one of the few herbs that cannot be dried successfully, so use fresh leaves if possible. Young leaves are the sweetest so it is best to sow plenty of seeds to ensure a constant crop and remove the flowers to encourage leaf growth. If using dried leaves pulverise them to release the full aroma. Basil thrives in a sunny position and light, rich soil, but do not over-water.

Ocimum basilicum 'Purpurescens
PURPLE BASIL

This attractive variety of basil is useful to grow as a pot herb or to add colour to salads and vinegars.

Origanum onites
MARJORAM, POT MARJORAM, FRENCH MARJORAM

Marjoram is a sweetly scented herb often used in Mediterranean cookery. It grows as a small bush with tiny green leaves and pink flowers.

Fresh or dried leaves give flavour to salads and jellies as well as meat dishes and the flowers make attractive additions to many decorative arrangements. Marjoram can be air dried in bunches and keeps its flavour and aroma well. Use it in dried herb sachets to scent clothes and repel insects. Marjoram can be grown from seed in the spring and prefers a rich, well-drained soil. It is a suitable herb for growing in pots on its own or in tubs and window boxes with a selection of other herb plants with a compact growing habit.

Origanum vulgare 'Aureum'
GOLDEN MARJORAM

This variety of marjoram has golden-coloured leaves and a mild flavour. Its attractive colour makes it especially suitable for making decorative garlands and wreaths from fresh herbs.

Papaver somniferum
POPPY, OPIUM POPPY

Well-known for its medicinal properties, the opium poppy bears grey-green leaves and large flowers with papery petals in a wide range of colours from white to dark pink. There are also double-flowered forms

similar to peonies and carnations. The opium poppy is cultivated commercially to extract morphine. The dried seed-heads are attractive in floral arrangements and the tiny seeds are used to decorate breads and cakes. Poppies prefer to grow in a well-drained soil in full sun.

Pelargonium sp.
GERANIUM

Commonly called geraniums, there are many scented-leaved pelargoniums in a range of white, pinks and reds. They are evergreen perennials but are tender plants and are usually grown in containers so that

they can be moved inside. The leaves, with their scents of rose, apple, peppermint, orange, lemon, cinnamon and others, can be used fresh or dried in pot pourris. Oil is extracted for use in beauty preparations. The leaves are also used in salads and frosted to decorate cakes.

Petroselinum crispum
PARSLEY

Parsley is one of the most popular culinary herbs. There are two varieties – curly-leaved and flat-leaved. The plant ranges in height from dwarf types suitable for growing in pots to varieties which can reach 60 cm (2 ft) in height. Most of the flavour is in the stalks and parsley is used for sauces, soups and salads. The curly variety is most often used for garnishing dishes. Parsley prefers a sunny position and rich, moist soil.

Rosa sp.
ROSE

The fragrant rose has been used for centuries for many medicinal, culinary and cosmetic purposes. Fresh and dried buds, flower heads and petals are used for their colour and scent in pot pourris, scent sachets and skin preparations.

Oil is also extracted and the damask rose and cabbage rose are the main species used for aromatherapy purposes. Petals are also used for teas, jams, vinegars and wines. Rosehip syrup, made from the berries of the wild rose, is rich in vitamin C. Roses prefer a well-drained soil in an open, sunny or partially shaded position.

Rosmarinus officinalis
ROSEMARY

Rosemary is a strong-flavoured, hardy evergreen herb. With its aromatic, needle-shaped, blue-green leaves, it is easily identified. In late spring and during mild weather it produces blue, pink or white flowers. Rosemary has many uses as a flavouring in food and liqueurs and in decorative arrangements, pot pourris and beauty treatments. When dried, the leaves keep their flavour well. It grows best in light, dry soil and prefers a sheltered position. It is more fragrant if grown on a chalky soil.

Rumex acetosa
SORREL, BROAD-LEAVED SORREL

Sorrel belongs to the dock family. With its broad leaves it is similar to spinach in appearance, taste and cooking methods. It will grow to about 60 cm (2 ft) in height, producing reddish-green flowers in midsummer. Sorrel is often used to flavour mayonnaise and sauce to accompany fish, in tarts and soups, and the young leaves can be eaten raw in salads. In spring the leaves are almost tasteless, but develop in acidity as the season progresses. Sorrel will grow in most types of soil and situations.

Rumex scutatus
BUCKLER-SHAPED SORREL, FRENCH SORREL

This variety of sorrel has a slightly milder flavour than Broad-leaved sorrel. Its attractive leaves make it suitable for growing in window boxes with a selection of other culinary herbs.

Salvia officinalis
SAGE

There are many varieties of green sage, of which Garden sage is the most common. It is a strongly flavoured, aromatic evergreen shrub which can grow to a height of 120 cm (4 ft). Other varieties include Golden sage, Pineapple sage and Red or Purple sage. Sage leaves are widely used both fresh and dried for culinary, decorative and aromatic purposes. Sage will grow in almost any well-drained soil in a sunny position.

Sambucus nigra
ELDERFLOWER

Elder is a hardy deciduous shrub or tree. There are two varieties – the European elder grows to a height of 7 m (22 ft), while the smaller, shrubbier American variety reaches a height of 4 m (12 ft). Its creamy white flowers bloom in early summer and produce a beautiful scent. They are used for skin and hair preparations and for vinegars, wines and

cordials. The ripe berries can be made into wine or used in jam-making.

Santolina chamaecyparissus
SANTOLINA, COTTON LAVENDER

Santolina is a hardy evergreen shrub with aromatic silver-green, feathery leaves and small, yellow, button flowers. Often planted as hedging, santolina grows to a height of 60 cm (2 ft). Its leaves and flowers may be used fresh in decorative arrangements or dried in scent sachets and pot pourris. The pungent scent repels moths and insects. Santolina prefers a sandy, well-drained soil in an open sunny position.

Saponaria officinalis
SOAPWORT, BOUNCING BET, SOAPROOT, WILD SWEET WILLIAM

Soapwort is an attractive herb with large, pale pink flowers. It usually reaches to a height of 60 cm (2 ft), but can grow to 1.5 m (5 ft). This herb is not scented but the leaves and root macerated in water produce a

gentle lather excellent for cleaning delicate fabrics. Dried soapwort can be used to make hair shampoo. It thrives in a sunny position and moist soil.

Symphytum officinale
COMFREY

Comfrey is a member of the borage family. It is a hardy perennial with long, coarse grey-green leaves and produces blue or cream flowers throughout the summer. A tall, spreading plant which grows to a height of 60–90 cm (2–3 ft), it seeds itself. Traditionally used in poultices to alleviate bruises, comfrey can be added to herbal bath gel. Comfrey will grow in almost any type of well-drained, fertile soil.

Tanacetum parthenium
FEVERFEW, FLIRTWORT, BACHELOR'S BUTTONS

Feverfew has lacy yellow or green leaves and distinctive, daisy-like yellow and white flowers. The aromatic leaves are not often used in cooking due to their bitter taste, but they have been proved to be effective in curing headaches. The flowers make colourful decorations in fresh herbal arrangements. A hardy perennial, the plant reaches a height of 45–60 cm (18–24 in) and thrives in a well-drained, moist soil and full sunlight.

Tanacetum vulgare
TANSY, BUTTONS

Tansy is a hardy perennial with aromatic green leaves and clusters of yellow flowers. It is one of the taller herbs, reaching a height of 100–125 cm (3–4 ft). Tansy is grown mainly for decorative purposes and may also be used as a herbal insect repellant in sachets. Tansy will thrive in most types of soil.

Thymus citriodorus
LEMON THYME

This variety of thyme is sweetly scented and its small, bright green leaves have a mild citrus flavour. An evergreen herb, it grows to a height of 20–30 cm (8–12 in) and produces dark pink flowers in late summer. It is a popular culinary herb for poultry and stuffings and can also be used to flavour jellies and ice cream. Lemon thyme prefers a dry, well-drained soil.

Thymus vulgaris
THYME, COMMON THYME, GARDEN THYME

There are many varieties of thyme and Common thyme is a cultivated form of the wild herb. This aromatic variety is a spreading evergreen perennial which grows to a maximum height of about 23 cm (9 in) and produces small mauve flowers in summer. Thyme is a

traditional ingredient of *bouquet garni*. It is also used fresh or dried as a flavouring in jellies and vinegars, and decoratively in pot pourris, wreaths and garlands. Thyme prefers a sunny position and will grow in any well-drained soil.

Tilia × vulgaris
LIME, LINDEN BLOSSOM

The lime or linden is a deciduous tree with glossy green heart-shaped leaves. It grows to a height of 15.25 m (50 ft) and produces heavily scented yellow flowers. When picked young, the dried blossom can be used to make a popular relaxing herbal tea. The dried flowers and linden oil can also be used in pot pourris. The lime tree prefers a well-drained soil in a sunny position.

Vanilla planifolia
VANILLA

The vanilla is a tender climbing plant that grows in tropical, humid conditions, reaching a height of 12 m (40 ft). It has long, leathery leaves and produces yellow or orange flowers. The flowers are followed by long, aromatic fruit pods called beans which, when dried, can be used to flavour a wide variety of foodstuffs from ice cream to cakes and confectionery. Vanilla oil is also used in perfumes and pot pourris and in scented candles.

Viola odorata
VIOLET, SWEET VIOLET

Violet is a small perennial with heart-shaped leaves and dainty sweet-scented violet or white flowers. An oil can be extracted from the flowers and the flowers used to flavour liqueurs, vinegars and confectionery. They may also be used in posies and pot pourris. When crystallised or frosted the flowers make an attractive decoration for cakes and fruit salads. Violet prefers a humus-rich soil and semi-shade.

Zingiber officinale
GINGER

Ginger is a tender creeping plant that grows in tropical conditions, reaching a height of 1–1.2 m (3–4 ft). It has reed-like stems with lance-shaped leaves which grow from rhizomes or roots. The roots may be used fresh or ground to provide a warming, spicy flavour in cakes, biscuits, beers, ales and wine. When ground, ginger can be used to scent pomanders and pot pourris. Ginger requires a rich soil and a hot environment.

Herb Sources

Fresh Herb Suppliers

Iden Croft Herbs
Frittenden Road
Staplehurst
Kent
TN12 0DH
Tel 0580 891432

Hollington Nurseries Limited
Woolton Hill
Newbury
Berkshire
RG15 9XT
Tel 0635 253908

Lathbury Park Herbs
Newport Pagnell
Buckinghamshire
MK16 8LD
Tel 0908 618101

Norfolk Lavender Limited
Caley Mill
Heacham
King's Lynn
Norfolk
PE13 7JE
Tel 0485 570384

Dried Flowers and Dried Herbs

Goldherb
Unit 7
Kestrel Close
Bridgend Industrial Estate
Mid Glamorgan
CF31 3RW
(Post only)

Focal Flowers
17 Cross Flatts Avenue
Beeston
Leeds
LS11 7BE
Tel 0532 774001

Simply Dried
Freepost
Kingsbridge
Devon
TQ7 1BR
(Freepost only)

The Flower Loft
E4 Marabout
Dorchester
Dorset
DT1 1YA
Tel/Fax 0305 251853

The HOP Shop
Castle Farm
Shoreham
Sevenoaks
Kent
TN14 7UB
Tel 0959 523219
Fax 0959 524220

The Flower Barn
37 Hill Lane
Barnham
West Sussex
PO22 0BL
Tel 0243 553490

Ribbons

Ribbon Designs
42 Lakeview
Edgeware
HA8 7RU
Tel 081 958 4966

Teas

The Dury Tea & Coffee
Company
3 New Row
London
WC2N 4LH
Tel 071 836 1960

Whittards of Chelsea
73 Northcote Road
London
SW11 6PJ
Tel 071 924 1888

Essential Oils and Cosmetic Bases

Aromatherapy Associates
68 Maltings Place
Bagleys Lane
London
SW16 2BY
Tel 071 371 9878

Culpeper Ltd
Hadstock Road
Linton
Cambridge
CB1 6NJ
Tel 0223 894054
Fax 0223 893104

G Baldwin
173 Walworth Road
London
SE7
Tel 071 703 5550

Pure Essentials
Ganders Close
Brandon Road
Newark
Nottingham
NG23 5BY
Tel 0636 626168

Sandra Day
4 Healey Hall Mews
Shawclough Road
Rochdale
OL12 7HB
Tel 0706 356328

Candle Waxes

Candle Makers and Suppliers
28 Blythe Road
London
W14 0HA
Tel 071 602 4031

Diddy Box
132/134 Belmont Road
Bolton
BL1 7AN
Tel 0204 595610

Fred Aldous
PO Box 135
37 Lever Street
Manchester 1
M60 1UX
Tel 061 236 2477

Neals Yard
5 Golden Cross
Cornmarket Street
Oxford
OX1 3EU
Tel 0865 245436

Craft Materials

Panduro Hobby
Westway House
Transport Avenue
Brentford
Middlesex
TW8 9HF
Tel 0474 708182

Fred Aldous
PO Box 135
37 Lever Street
Manchester 1
M60 1UX
Tel 061 236 2477

Diddy Box
132/134 Belmont Road
Bolton
BL1 7AN
Tel 0204 595610

Terracotta Pots/Dried Wreaths

Goldherb
Unit 7
Kestrel Close
Bridgend Industrial Estate
Mid Glamorgan
CF31 3RW
(Post only)

The Flower Loft
E4 Marabout
Dorchester
Dorset
DT1 1YA
Tel/Fax 0305 251853

The HOP Shop
Castle Farm
Shoreham
Sevenoaks
Kent
TN14 7UB
Tel 0959 523219
Fax 0959 524220

Florist Sundries/ Paints/Glue Guns

The Flower Loft
E4 Marabout
Dorchester
Dorset
DT1 1YA
Tel/Fax 0305 251853

Goldherb
Unit 7
Kestrel Close
Bridgend Industrial Estate
Mid Glamorgan
CF31 3RW
(Post only)

Panduro Hobby
Westway House
Transport Avenue
Brentford
Middlesex
TW8 9HF
Tel 0474 708182

Fred Aldous
PO Box 135
37 Lever Street
Manchester 1
M60 1UX
Tel 061 236 2477

Diddy box
132/134 Belmont Road
Bolton
BL1 7AN
Tel 0204 595610

Other Useful Addresses

The Herb Society
134 Buckingham Palace Road
London
SW1W 9SA
Tel 071 823 5584

The Royal Horticultural Society
Wisley Garden Centre
Woking
Surrey
GU23 6QB
Tel 0483 211113

Chelsea Physic Garden
66 Royal Hospital Road
London
SW3 4HS
(The garden has a large herbal section)
Tel 071 352 5464

The National Institute of
Medical Herbalists
9 Palace Gate
Exeter
Devon
EX1 1JA
Tel 0392 426022

School of Phytotherapy
Bucksteep Manor
Boodle Street Green
Hailsham
East Sussex
BN27 4RJ
Tel 0323 833812

Courses

Institute of Clinical
Aromatherapy
9 Papyrus Road
Werrington Business Park,
Werrington,
Peterborough,
Cambridgeshire
PE4 5DH
Tel 0733 321101

Index

A

alcohol 178
allspice essential oil *100*
almond & rose hand cream 186-7
angelica *10, 59, 79*, 136, *172*, 208
  cake 59
  candied 59, 79, 207
aniseed 206
applemint *31, 56, 192*, 212
  angel food cake 56
apricot: ice cream 49
  moisturiser 194-5
aromatherapy 94, 217
artemisia *see* southernwood

B

baking 32-7
baldness 196
ball, red rose 119
balm 204
  foot bath 189
barrels 154, *156*
basil *11, 25, 42*, 78, 141, 146, *149*, 204, 207, 212
  in a basket 149
  pesto sauce 42
  purple basil *149*, 212
  roast pepper salad with 25
baskets 121, 149, 157
bath additives 170-5, 204
bay *52*, 104, 112, 124, 132, 160, *182*, 211
  dried 204, 205
  foot bath 189
  hair tonic 200-1
  tree 116-7
beauty preparations 190-5
benzoin tincture *182*
bergamot *94, 110, 178*, 212
  essential oil 101, 178
berries 160
borage 204, 206, 207, 209
bouquet garni 72, 112
box 160, *200*, 209
  hair tonic 200-1
  tree, conical 167
boxes, wooden *152-3*, 154-6
brandy 71
breads *33*, 34, 36
bubble bath gel 172-3
bunches/bundles *10*, 130-5
  Christmas tree decorations 164
  insect-repellent 85
  on twig ring 129
  rosemary, marjoram & thyme 135

butter, herb 207

C

cakes *10*, 52-9, 207
candles 216-7
  decorated 165
  scented 99
candying 79, 207
caraway *32*, 206, 209
  rye oaten bread 36
carnation 78
carrot 192
cassia oil 94
cedarwood *82, 100*, 209
  essential oil 100
chamomile 60, *63*, 104, 184, 186, *188*, 192, 196, 198, 209
  hand gel 188-9
  tisane 63
cheese: & thyme scones 37
  blended with herbs 38
  soft, with herbs *38*, 43-4
  straws, poppyseed 75
chervil 21, 112, 204, 207, 208
  egg & lemon soup with 20
chilli: tortilla chips 35
  wood shaving mixture 96-7
chives *18*, 44, 78, *151, 158*, 204, 207, 208
  in painted pot 151
  soft cheese with *38*, 43
Christmas decorations 160-7
chutney 74-5
cinnamon 130
  with roses 113, 134-5
citrus: herb liqueur 69
  splash 178-9
cleanser, mint 193
colognes 176-83
comfrey 214
containers: pots 136-43
  wooden 152-9
cordials 66-71
coriander *14, 21, 75*, 112, 206, 210
  chutney with 74-5
  Thai fish soup with 20
crystallised flowers 207
cushions 88, *90*
  hop-filled 92-3

D

dill *40*, 204, 206, 208
  & mustard sauce 40
dried herbs 204, 205, 216
  displays 111, 113-21, 124, 160, 204

drinks 60-5
drying: herbs 110, 111, 130, 204-5
  oranges 96

E

eau de cologne 183
egg: & soapwort shampoo 199
  soup 20-1
elder *70*
elderflower 78, 186, *188*, 192, 214
  cordial 70
  hand gel 188-9
  rinse 198
emulsions 192
essential oils 82, 94-101, 104, 114, 170, 173, 176, 184, 216
eucalyptus *104*, 184, 210
  leaf garland 121

F

fennel 184, 192, *195*, 204, *205*, 206, 210
  bronze fennel 141
feverfew *128*, 215
fish soup with coriander 20-1
fixative 88, 102
fleas 87
flies 82, 87
flowers: harvesting 204
  preserving 206, 207
foam, floral 114, *115*, 124, 126
focaccia, rosemary 34
foot bath 189
foot cream 187
fragrances 176-83
freezing herbs 112, 206
frosted geranium leaves 55
fruit: dried 96, 130
  pyramid 162

G

garden containers 136-43, 152-9
garlands 124-9
garlic *17, 42*, 78, 207, 208
  soft cheese with *38*, 43
  tortilla chips 35
gazpacho with herbs 17
geranium *55*, 104, 144, 146, *151*, 184, 186, 192, 213
  layer cake 54
  leaves, frosted 55, 207
gifts, edible 72-9
ginger *75*, 215
glue-gun 114, 217
goat cheese & strawberry salad 28

golden marjoram *26, 126*, 213
  rose garland 126
growing herbs: indoors 144-51
  outdoors 136-43, 152-9

H

hair rinses 198, 201
hair tonic 200-1
hand cream 186-7
hand gel 188-9
harvesting herbs 204
hawthorn *66*, 210
  may blossom brandy 71
heart, pink rose 118-9
heliotrope 140
helxine in painted pot 151
hop 210-1
  cushion 92-3
horsetail 196
hyssop 85, 104, *108, 110*, 111, 211

I

ice cubes 206
ices 46-51
indoor gardening 144-51
insect repellents 82-7

J

jasmine 99, 211
  tea 62, 63
jelly, herb 76-7

L

lavender *51*, 78, *84*, 85, 87, 104, 108, *124, 129, 130*, 172, *183*, 184, 186, 192, 211
  bottles 84-5
  bundle, dried 132-3
  essential oil 94
  foot cream 187
  growing 138, 140
  ice cream 52
  pot pourri 107
  sachets 88, 91
  wreath 128
leaves: frosted 55
  herb pot pourri 104-5
lemon balm *64, 142, 143*, 211
  lemonade 64
  tisane 63
lemon thyme *51, 170*, 215
  sorbet 50-1
lemon verbena *52, 77*, 104, 138, *170, 179*, 208
  & orange splash 178-9
lemonade, lemon balm 64

lime (linden blossom) *102*, 104, 215
  skin freshener 182-3
liqueurs 66-71
lovage 136

M

marigold 78, 104, *106*, 184, 186, 192, 209
  & apricot ice cream 49
  pot pourri 106
marjoram 111, *114*, *152*, 159, 204, 212
  & poppy basket 121
  rosemary & thyme bundle 135
  see also golden marjoram
may blossom *see* hawthorn
mayonnaise 38
Mediterranean mixed pot 140
melissa *see* lemon balm
melon with mint & violet *22*, 30-1
meringues, violet 57
mesclun 30-1
mice 10, 82
mint *17*, *87*, 136, 204, 206, 207, 211
  cleanser 193
  eau de cologne mint *193*
  ginger mint 60
  melon with 30
  pineapple mint *142*
moisturiser 194-5
moths 82, 85, 87
mustard & dill sauce 40

N

nasturtium 78
nettle 196

O

oatmeal scrub 170, 175
oil: bath 173
  flavoured 72
orange: dried 96
  moisturiser 194-5
  peel, dried 90
  splash 178-9
orangeflower water 178, *194*
orris root 87, 102

P

paints 150-1, 152, 159, 217
parsley *29*, *40*, *144*, 204, 206, 207, 213
  curly-leaved *112*, *146-7*, 151
pasta salad, tricolor 26
pelargoniums in box 156

pennyroyal 87, 212
peppermint *28*, 60, 82, 184, 212
peppers: chutney 74-5
  salad 25
perfumes 176-83
pesto sauce 42
pillows 88
pink 210
pomegranate pyramid 162
poppy *134*, 213
  & marjoram basket 121
  seeds 75, 206
posies 108-13, 162
pot-holder, hanging 146-7
pot pourri 102-7, 204
potato & sorrel soup 18-9
pots 136-43, 150-1, 217
preserves 72-9
preserving herbs 204-7
primrose 78
purée, herb 38, *39*

R

ribbon 216, *127*
rose *46*, *71*, 85, 104, *114*, 124, 162, 172, *180*, 186, 192, 213
  ball, red 119
  brandy 71
  crystallised petals 207
  garland 126
  hand cream 186-7
  heart, pink 118-9
  ice cream 48
  layer cake 54
  perfume 180
  posy 113
  pot pourri, red 105
  steam treatment 195
  stook 134-5
  tea 62
  wreath *11*, *127*
  see also rosewater
rosemary *34*, *78*, 87, 104, 111, 124, 132, 138, *160-2*, 172, *176*, *183*, *187*, 196, 204, 213
  bundle 135
  focaccia 34
  foot cream 187
  rinse 201
rosewater 190
  & witch hazel toner 192

S

sachets 88, *90*, 204
  bath 174
  insect-repellent 87
  lavender 91

sage 104, 108, 111, 112, 124, 132, *136*, 159, *187*, 204, 214
  foot cream 187
  growing 141, 143
  pineapple sage 104
  red sage tisane 63
  rinse 201
salad burnet 206
salads 22-31, 204
salting herbs 207
sandalwood 82
santolina 143, 214
sauces 40, 42
savory 104, 111
scones, cheese & thyme 37
scrub, bath 175
seeds, dried 206
shampoo 199
skin freshener 190
  lime 182-3
soap, pure 172
soapwort *196*, 198, 214
  & egg shampoo 199
sorbet, lemon thyme 50
sorrel *18*, *19*, 214
  & potato soup 18-9
  French sorrel *159*, 214
soups 14-21
southernwood 85, *87*, 108, 111, 208-9
spices 130, 160
  sweet powder 90
splash 178-9
steam treatment, rose 195
stooks 130, 132
  cinnamon & rose 134-5
strawberry: & cheese salad 28
  plants *159*
sweet cicely 28
sweet powder 88, 90, 93
sweet woodruff 60, *65*, 172, 210
  summer cup 65

T

tabbouleh salad 29
table settings 162
tansy *87*, 215
tarragon *44*, *69*, 204, 207, 209
  vinegar 78, *79*, 207
teas 60-3, 204, 216
  rose petal 62
thyme 37, 78, 88, 104, 111, *112*, 124, 136, *138*, *154*, *160*, *175*, 204, 215
  & cheese scones 37
  essential oil 94
  golden thyme 159

in fruit box 154-5
  pot, with pebbles 138-9
  rosemary & marjoram bundle 135
  silver thyme 108
  see also lemon thyme
tisanes 63, 204
tomato chutney 74-5
toner 190, 192
tortilla chips 35
tree 116-7, 167
  Christmas, decorations 164
trug, violas in 157
tubs *152*
tussie-mussies *see* posies
twig ring 129

V

vanilla 215
  & rose perfume 180
vine wreath 128
vinegar, herb 78-9, 207
viola *57*, *157*
  in trug 157
violet 78, 215
  crystallised 207
  melon with 30
  meringues 57
vodka 69, 178

W

walnut 211
  foot bath 189
willow 196
window boxes 158-9
witch hazel 190
  toner 192
wood: outdoor containers 152-9
  scenters 100
  shaving mixture 96-7
woodruff *see* sweet woodruff
wreaths *11*, 72, 124-9, 217
  lavender 128
  rose, on willow 127

Y

yarrow 196

Credits

Managing Editor: Jo Finnis

Contributor: Geraldine Christy

Contributing and consultant editor: Josephine Bacon

Additional editorial work: Sue Wilkinson

Design: Jill Coote; Nigel Duffield

Photography: Di Lewis and The Garden Picture Library pages 136-7 (Linda Burgess), 139 (John Glover), 140-1 (John Glover), 142-3 (John Glover), 154 top right, 157 top right (Brian Carter), 158 (Jon Bouchier), 159 top right (John Glover), 202-3 (Marianne Majerus), 204-5 (Lamontagne), 205 (Mayer/Le Scanff), 206 (Mayer/Le Scanff), 206-7; Harry Smith Horticultural Photographic Collection pages 152, 156 right; herb portraits by Stonecastle Graphics Ltd

Colour illustrations: Nicola Gregory

Typesetting: SX Composing, Rayleigh, Essex

Production: Ruth Arthur; Sally Connolly; Neil Randles; Karen Staff; Jonathan Tickner; Matthew Dale

Production Director: Gerald Hughes